Rajashekhara Reddy

Tragic End of a Charismatic Chief Minister

About the Author

Mahadevan P. Rao (b. 1962) is a well-known freelance journalist and political analyst from Hyderabad. He writes regularly for various newspapers and magazines. Also, he has participated in some national and international conferences on media-related issues.

Rajashekhara Reddy

Tragic End of a Charismatic Chief Minister

Mahadevan P. Rao

Epitome Books
New Delhi

First published 2009

Published by

Epitome Books

B-65 Mansaram Park
Near Nawada Metro Station
New Delhi – 110 059-06

Phone: 011-2537 1324
Fax: +91-11-2537 1323

Email: info@epitomebooks.com
Web: www.epitomebooks.com

Cataloging in Publication Data--DK
Courtesy: D.K. Agencies (P) Ltd. <docinfo@dkagencies.com>

Rao, Mahadevan P., 1962-
Rajashekhara Reddy : tragic end of a charismatic chief minister / Mahadevan P. Rao.
p. cm.
Y.S. Rajasekhar Reddy, 1949-2009, former chief minister of Andhra Pradesh, India.

ISBN 13: 978-93-80297-13-2 ISBN 10: 93-80297-13-0

1. Rajasekhar Reddy, Y. S., 1949-2009. 2. Politicians--India--Andhra Pradesh--Biography. 3. Andhra Pradesh (India)--Politics and government--21st century. 4. Community development--India--Andhra Pradesh. I. Title.

DDC 954.84092 22

Printed at Salasar Imaging Systems, Delhi - 35

Preface

Controversy was Y S Rajasekhara Reddy's constant companion in politics—as one who represented violence-prone Cuddapah in Parliament, and the legislative Assembly since the late 1970s. But electoral triumphs buttressed by populist schemes transformed it all for the Andhra CM. In his death, the Congress has lost its strongest regional face in recent memory.

Reddy's 2004 triumph over old friend and formidable rival Chandrababu Naidu helped the Congress wrest power from the Telugu Desam Party (TDP) in the state and the National Democratic Alliance at the Centre. A slew of sops and schemes helped him extinguish two challenges in one go: Mr Naidu and the Naxals who exploited the TDP's urban-centric approach in the countryside. His people-oriented programmes even demolished the demand for Telangana as a poll plank.

In a state where successive droughts during the TDP rule led to farmer suicides, Reddy, born into the family of a mason, provided rice for Rs 2 a kg for below poverty line families. He put revenues accruing from beneficiaries of first-generation reforms on the welfare route to arrange food, healthcare, insurance and rural employment for the marginalised.

He implemented schemes to help women and children and was known to encourage NGOs that wanted to work for the disadvantaged. That the Congress's success in Andhra was fathered solely by Reddy became evident with the party returning a larger chunk of MPs from the state in 2009 than it did in 2004. He defeated anti-incumbency despite a broken alliance with the Telangana Rashtra Samithi (on the Telangana issue) and the Left (on the Indo-US nuclear deal).

Not only did he keep the promise made to Congress president Sonia Gandhi of adding to the party's 2004 tally of 29, he raised the score by four to win 33 seats. Formidable reputations routed in the process included that of matinee idol and Kappu chieftain—popular film star Chiranjeevi, whose Praja Rajyam Party proved to be just a flash in the pan.

But that's history now and so is Reddy, whose death has left a void no Andhra Congress politician, young or old, can fill in the short run. If there was one person who genuinely carried out the UPA's promise of delivering on its promises to the aam admi (common men), it would have been Reddy. But sadly, like so many others who held out great promise in politics, he is gone.

In this book, I have attempted to provide rich insights into the life and personality of Y.S. Rajashekhara Reddy. Taking a close look at his political journey, the book describes in detail how he led Congress to victory in Andhra Pradesh for two consecutive terms. It also makes a critical analysis of his development policies and programmes.

Content

1

His Life and Personality

Dr. Yeduguri Sandinti Rajasekhara Reddy, popularly known as YSR, was an astute politician and a charismatic mass leader who had carved for himself a niche in Andhra Pradesh politics by his exemplary devotion and dedication to the uplift of the downtrodden and neglected segments of society. Born on July 8, 1949, in Pulivendula in the backward Rayalaseema region, YSR has always struggled to secure the rights of the poor and the underprivileged. Son of late Y.S. Raja Reddy, a dynamic leader in his heyday, Rajasekhara Reddy evinced interest in politics right from his student days. While studying in M R Medical College, Gulbarga, Karnataka, he served as President of the Students Union. He was elected leader of the House Surgeon's Association in S V Medical College, Tirupati. After completing MBBS, he served as Medical Officer at the Jammalamadugu Mission Hospital for a brief period. In 1973, he established a 70-bed charitable hospital, named after his father late Y.S.Raja Reddy at Pulivendula. His family established one polytechnic and one degree college in Pulivendula, which were later handed over to the well-known Loyola group of institutions.

Rajasekhara Reddy's sound business acumen, entrepreneurial skills, and, above all, his transparency brought him laurels in the business arena. On the flip side, his success also brought him many adversaries, political and otherwise, who were desperately looking for a shred of evidence to prove umpteen charges against him. In the end, their mud-slinging did not yield a single point that could paint the mass leader in bad light. In fact, his detractors became red-faced, as they had to swallow their words.

Groomed by a family deeply involved in public service, YSR entered active politics in 1978 and contested elections, four times to enter the State Legislative Assembly and an equal number of times to enter the Lower House of Parliament. A winner in all that he does, YSR won all the elections he contested. Even today his admirers exclaim: "He (YSR) defeats defeat." During his 25-year-long political career, YSR has served the people in multiple capacities, both in Government as well as in Party. He was President of the Andhra Pradesh Congress Committee (APCC) twice-1983-1985 and 1998-2000. During 1980-1983, he was a minister holding important portfolios related to Rural Development, Medical & Health and Education etc. From 1999 to 2004 he was the Leader of Opposition in the eleventh state assembly.

As a champion of the masses, his stentorian voice in the assembly, raised particularly during debates that sought to lend voice to the voiceless millions, forced the Government to retrace several anti-people steps it contemplated. YSR has been instrumental in orchestrating several mass struggles, while highlighting issues facing peasants, weavers, Dalits, youth and women. His relentless fight for clearance of pending irrigation projects, particularly in the backward Rayalaseema region, has earned for him a special place in the hearts of millions of farmers. His unremitting struggle against certain anti-people economic measures that were sought to be introduced in the name of "reforms", including the frequent increases in power tariff and indiscriminate privatization of public sector units, exalted him far above the street smart politicians.

Even as a novice in the legislature, YSR rallied all the Congress MLAs from the Rayalaseema region and led an indefinite hunger strike demanding solution to the water crisis.

He also led a.2 Paadayaatra from Lepakshi to Pothireddipadu in Kurnool district. The 14-day hunger strike of legislators under his leadership in August 2000 to register protest against the hike in power charges is still fresh in the memory of people. By systematically exposing the misdeeds of the then Government, both inside and outside the Assembly, YSR was playing his political role to the hilt. During mid-summer in 2003, he led an unprecedented 1400 Km long Paadayaatra covering all backward areas in the state to understand the ground realities of living conditions of the people there.

His Public Life

"I want to ensure that no field in Andhra Pradesh went dry without water; no farmer is driven to suicide for either crop failures or remunerative price for his produce; that no house of poor is in darkness for lack of electricity; and that no industry is closed for lack of infrastructure. My vision is for transforming the state into Haritandhrapradesh – a state where farm-fields always remain green and where the people wore bright smile on their face", said Chief Minister Dr.Y.S. Rajasekhara Reddy in his address to the Andhra Pradesh State Legislative Assembly. These are not words of a self-contended man, but that of a person who has risen from the bottom of the political pyramid in Andhra Pradesh, survived, created a niche for himself and got to the top post through continuous and painstaking efforts.

Dr. Reddy, popularly addressed by his admirers as YSR, was perhaps the first politician of Andhra Pradesh who strived through 25 years of public life and achieved his present position by dint of sheer hard work, and determined journey in State Congress. While majority of his contemporaries shifted loyalties, jumped fences and gulped their own public utterances and morphed their images, he stood like a rock, weathered all adverse situations and remained loyal to his beliefs with a charming and enchanting smile.

All visitors to his home and his office will be bowled out instantly for his humane approach laced with warm smile and his popular yet humble and simple opening remarks - "What Sir? Throughout his checkered political career of several ups and downs, Dr. Rajasekhar Reddy never lost sight of the poor farmer, women and the unemployed youth. He is totally dedicated to public service. He never believed in short cuts or adhocism-"I always aim to provide lasting solutions to burning problems faced by the society like poverty, diseases, illiteracy, unemployment and corruption. I insist with everyone that whatever be the time, resources and efforts needed one should always opt against adhocism and work for a final solutions", he used to say.

Early Years

Born on July 8, 1949, in Pulivendula village of Kadapa district in the backward Rayalaseema region in a farmer's family, Rajasekhara Reddy mingled with people and developed a taste for social service. He was always at the forefront for community welfare activities in the village. Fresh from his graduation in Medicine from Gulbarga Medical College in Karnataka he was attracted by the speeches and work of late prime minister and Congress President Mrs. Indira Gandhi. What attracted him more was Mrs. Gandhi's initiative-Garibi Hatao-aimed at eradicating poverty of the farmer.

Son of late Y.S. Raja Reddy, a social worker and former leader of Kadapa, Rajasekhara Reddy took to politics right from his student days. Raja Reddy's sound advice on moral based politics and to focus on welfare of farmers and women paid, good dividend.

Rajasekhara Reddy had set an electoral record of sorts. He had never seen defeat in any of the four assembly and four parliament elections he contested from Pulivendula and Kadapa constituencies respectively since 1978. He had never tasted defeat and was a winner all the time, say his ardent followers. Thus began his sojourn with the people of Andhra Pradesh 28 years ago, that Dr. Reddy had never looked back. In fact, Rajasekhara Reddy began the trend setting of Gandhian tool of Padayatras to redress public grievances way back in 1999-2000. Besides staging indefinite hunger strikes, he also undertook padayatra between Lepakshi in Anantpur to Pothireddipadu in Kurnool (150 kms) in early eighties to focus attention on drinking water and irrigation needs of the Rayalaseema districts.

Plunge into Politics

Dr. Reddy's political journey began at the bottom of the pyramid. He has risen to unequalled position and level through struggle, mass following and determination. He was a cabinet minister between1980-83 when Congress was in power in the state. He headed the state party as the President of the Andhra Pradesh Congress Committee during the crucial periods of 1983-85 and 1998-2000. He boosted the morale of the Congress workers in an era of discontent and growing influence of anti-Congressism spread by the Telugu Desam Party led by N.T. Ramarao. During both the general elections in the state YSR salvaged the image of the party from the battering of the emotion-packed TDP onslaught. After years of back seat driving in state affairs, Y S Rajasekhara Reddy took on the mantle with his political opponents. In 1999 he took on the TDP in a direct fight but the party missed power by a whisker.

Although it had sizable popular vote the party missed the numbers and in fitness of things YSR became the leader of Opposition in the state with 91 party legislators in the AP Assembly. It was during this period that Dr. Reddy gave voice and shape to his vision to fight for the redemption of the suffering of the masses. Both in the Assembly and outside it, YSR forcefully struck at the anti-people measures of the TDP led by N. Chandrababu Naidu. Under his leadership the Congress consolidated its alliance with the left parties and the MIM in the state and isolated the TDP and its saffron ally BJP.

One could say that it was ingenuous leadership of Dr. Reddy that helped the Congress to return to power in AP after a lapse of almost a decade and eclipse the TDP and the more than life image of its leader N Chandrababu Naidu that haunted the Congress Party .

Rajasekhara Reddy stunned the ruling party, the TDP, in the assembly and also outside with his forceful and well documented deliveries in the House. He steered the struggle against Naidu regime's power reforms without human face by bringing back anti-TDP and anti-BJP political forces together on a platform and staged an indefinite hunger strike against the government. He championed the cause of the masses and highlighted the issues of farmers, weavers, dalits, youth and women embracing the TDP regime day–in and day-out.

It goes to Dr. Reddy's credit that during his stint as an Opposition leader in the AP assembly his campaign exposed the lacunae in the Power Purchase Agreements (PPA's). YSR also took up the cause of farmers' suicides in his correspondence with the National Human Rights Commission and thus won their confidence and built a case for giving them economic assistance including 'free power'.

His Personality

The hallmark of all great men is simplicity in thought and deed. These elements were profoundly and abundantly resplendent in Dr. Reddy throughout his political journey. A loving father, caring husband, popular mass leader, versatile administrator and above all a good Christian, YSR was the embodiment of a mature and astute Indian politician who dared to have a vision of his own in spite of heavy odds and adversaries all around him. As a trusted lieutenant of the Congress party both when out of power and also while in power, Dr. Reddy was the most revered and admired contemporary Andhra politician in the country. He had brought a sea change in the functioning of the state bureaucracy and his own CMO by infusing simple and effective guidelines, where hypocrisy and hyped up publicity mongering have no room.

Despite huge personal risks after the Maoists walked out of peace talks (they refuse to give up arms even while pursing peace) Dr. Reddy met a minimum of 100 visitors without any appointment every day at his daily durbar at his camp office. "They come from hundreds of miles to see me and tell their sufferings. I have no hesitation to give such people a minimum of 60 minutes everyday in spite of my busy schedule", he had instructed his staff.

His modesty was reflected even in his interaction with senior bureaucrats. YSR relaxed the regimentation. "I don't need the chief secretary to brief me in person. It is okay if tells me the days development in tele conference", he says. So no early morning blues for officials who can go ahead with their daily chore of administration without wasting any time. He was perhaps the only Chief Minister who did not have any hang ups on inhibitions on personal likes and dislikes. He was also the one who did not insist on a traffic blocks for his caravan.

Citizens of Hyderabad were relieved that there would be no more the hours of waiting and traffic bottlenecks to facilitate a CM's motorcade. "After all we are part of the society, and earlier decisions to stall traffic for CM's caused enormous wastage of fuel and also valuable time of the commuters", he said. Dr. Reddy and his family believed in simple living. YSR always took time out for entertainment and relaxation and weekends. "Administration is not one man show. It is a combination of collective decisions and actions. I believe and want every government employee to feel responsible and do his part faithfully. I can not be all in all or all in one. My job is to give a direction. I am confident that every one else will deliver their part of the function. I do not believe in empty sloganeering or projections of working for 18 hours a day etc".

The chief minister believed in calling a spade, a spade .He advocated against hiding facts or white washing statistics. "The truth will come out one day and instead of carrying the stigma through out our lifetime let us dismiss it as a day-to-day issue", he said. What perhaps his strongest point of his personality was YSR's warmth and a friendly smile on a 24x7 basis. One could hardly ever find him pensive or worked up in public. His warm smile had always disarmed many of his opponents and media critics. "Many come to him with complaints and critical questions. But his friendly appearance totally envelopes everyone and they leave without any heart burning" says Suridu, one of Dr. Reddy's life time personal associate.

His Mission

From the beginning Dr. Reddy had been a champion of reforms with a human face. It is this humane principle that prompted him to take pioneering steps to ensure delivery services, benefits and initiatives for total redressal of the problem. Within an hour of his taking oath as chief minister at Lal Bahadur Stadium in May 2004, he announced waiver of electricity dues of poor farmers and also Free power for agriculture. There after followed his program to permanently eradicate rural poverty and give assured water to all cultivable lands in the state.

The Indira Kranti Patham, Jalayajnam, Indiramma, Bhoo Yajnam, Bhoo Bharati are among the flagship programs of YSR government aimed at eradicating rural and urban poverty, give land to landless, houses to all and also construct irrigation projects to provide assured water to all lands. Rajiv Swagriha is yet another project that Dr.Y.S.R. launched, to see that every middle income group family would own a house. Under Arogya Sri programme, a novel health insurance scheme is introduced for the BPL families, so that the poor could get surgery treatment worth upto Rs.2 lakhs, while the govt. would pay the total premium. "We are taking external loans for productive purposes and raising internal resources also" says YSR replying to oft sought clarification on how he raised funds for all projects.

Dr. Reddy had not relegated social welfare sector in his zeal for key programs like free-power to agriculture, massive Irrigation projects, land distribution to landless and Housing for poor. "The SC/ST, Minorities and women besides elderly persons get a larger share of the budget than in the past. We have not forgotten our principle duties to the society-primary health, primary education, in our pursuit for achieving sustainable development of Industry, Agriculture, small scale sector, IT, BT and textiles" he told the global audience at the ADB meetings in Hyderabad during May 2006.

His Pastime

Dr. Reddy was one of those few politicians of India who practise what they believe in–to serve the people to the last breath. But for the little time he gave his family and friends, Rajasekhara Reddy always found pleasure to be with people and understand their problems. He traveled across the state for 5500 kms spread over 20 days between April 5 to 20 to consolidate the gains of his earlier Padayatra. Almost an year ago he had walked 1500 kms on foot to understand the suffering of the people.

As an opposition leader and also as a MLA and MP and Party president, Dr. Reddy spent most of his time in visiting villages and districts all over the state. As a chief minister too he continued the practice with a dual purpose. He wanted feedback from the people for his new initiatives so that he could take corrective steps to ensure their acceptability and benefits to larger sections of the population.

Hence he coined district tours after his beloved leader Rajiv Gandhi- Rajiv Palle Bata and Rajiv Nagara Bata to elicit public response for his administration. Traveling 200 miles by road for atleast two days a week became his lifestyle for over two years. After completing the village rounds, he continued the exercise to acclimatize with the people in semi-urban towns and cities of the state. His 'Bata' tours became so famous that several departments also coined their campaigns after the Chief Ministers ingenious program to address their message for farmers, women, youth, school children, industrial workers, HIV/AIDS and Polio vaccines.

His Approach

YSR is known for his no-nonsense approach to everything in life. He did not mince words and always believed in a direct approach to the problems instead of delay or postponing them. Dr. Reddy made it clear to everyone that although promotion of agriculture and farmers welfare was very dear to his heart he had no bias against new and emerging technologies like IT and BT etc. His government has promoted the PPP platform to introduce several initiatives in the Infrastructure sector.

Soon after assumption of office he spelled out his agenda to the bureaucrats and urged them to ensure its successful implementation. "We are all here to serve the people. Let us do it to the best of our ability" he told them. Similar were his approach to win over the support and confidence of legislators of all hues including those of his party. "My doors are open to all for problems of people at any time of the day" he told them and urged them to make best of use of the opportunity for the betterment of the society. Dr. Reddy's humane approach to problems of the poor always earned him laurels and blessings of everyone. He strived day and night to put prime minister Pandit Jawaharlal Nehru's words into action. "I want to wipe out every tear from the eyes of all poor in this nation" Nehru had said in his address to the nation on the eve of first independence day celebration.

His Testimonies

Dr. Reddy was not just a man of the masses but also a fine tuned strategist and mature administrator. Within months of taking over as Chief Minister of Andhra Pradesh, he brought financial discipline in his administration which earned him kudos from all including the World Bank. Pessimists who cried hoarse that the state would not be able to raise any funds for its programs and drive investors away from AP in view of farmers free power initiative are now taken aback that almost every financial institution was keen to invest in AP's projects and also in the state.

The president of World Bank Dr. Wolfowitz was all praise for his human face approach to economic reforms. Although the apex bank had initial resistance to fund AP program in view of its free power to farmer's initiative, it came around later. The bank has continued its anti-poverty and other reforms program funding. "The states application for funding the irrigation works is also receiving WB's positive consideration "says the WB spokesman.

The President of Asian Development Bank Mr. Haruhiko Kuroda was full of praise for the development initiatives of the Dr. Reddy's administration. He was happy that all the borrowings were now being utilized in the productive and developmental activities instead of establishment expenditure.

A glowing testimony to Dr. Reddy's political and economic acumen came from another global dignitary, the then President of United States George W Bush. During his recent visit to Andhra Pradesh, the US President paid hearty kudos to the initiatives of Dr. Reddy's administration for the prosperity of farmers. "I am happy that the reforms are continued with human face", the President had told the Chief Minister.

The Prime Minister Dr. Manmohan Singh and AICC President Sonia Gandhi have recognized the Dr. Reddy's proactive and people friendly measures and have hailed AP as a role model state for emulation in anti-poverty and sustainable development initiatives. The Prime minister described Dr. Reddy as a visionary who strived to bridge rural and urban divide in AP. The state has been chosen for launch of the flagship anti-poverty schemes of UPA government like National rural employment guarantee scheme.

Religious Background

Reddy is a second-generation Christian. His father, Raja Reddy, while serving in the military in Burma came across Christian missionaries and although a firm believer in Hinduism soon converted to Christianity. After returning to India, he was despised by his own caste folk and shunted out of the village. By this time, missionaries in India were leaving the shores and handing over the administration of the Church to Indians. It was in 1947 that the Church of South India was formed. Raja Reddy began to attend the Church Services of this congregation.

The Church of South India is headquartered in Chennai with dioceses throughout South India. Y.S. Vivekananda Reddy, the brother of Rajasekhara Reddy, is a fund-raiser and member of the local committee of the Bible Society of India headquartered in Bangalore with auxiliaries in each state. Likewise, Rajasekhara Reddy's sister is into conducting Bible classes for women. Rajasekhara's son-in-law is a global evangelist speaker.

2

His Political Journey

Y.S. Rajasekhara Reddy's initiation into politics began in Karnataka when he won the election to become the students' union president of Mahadevappa Rampure Medical College (MRMC) in Gulbarga, where he did his MBBS from 1966 to 1972. Dr. Reddy's association with Karnataka dates back to 1958 when his father Y.S. Raja Reddy, a contractor from Pulivendala in Kadapa district of Andhra Pradesh, came to Bellary after bagging the contract for construction of a high-level canal on the right bank of the Tungabhadra Reservoir.

Dr. Reddy was a student of St. John's High School in the Fort area in Bellary for three years. After his schooling in Bellary, Dr. Reddy went to Vijayawada to join Loyola College and completed his Intermediate there. As he was keen on studying medicine, Dr. Reddy returned to Bellary to complete his first year B.Sc. (which was then compulsory to join MBBS) at Veerashaiva College.

He later returned to his hometown of Pulivendula in Kadapa district, where he ran a medical practice for five years. Till he entered the poll fray from Pulivendula, which he represented in the Assembly since 1980. He was also elected to the Lok Sabha from Kadapa for four terms.

He was a minister in the cabinet of T Anjaiah between 1980-83, after which the TDP came to power. He was president of the Andhra Pradesh Congress Committee (APCC) from 1983 to1985, and again from 1998 to 2000. From 1999 to 2004, he was the Leader of Opposition in the 11th Assembly.

He Had Rocky Start in Cong, with Rajiv

One of the most admired Congress chief ministers, Y S Rajasekhara Reddy had a less than smooth relationship with the party high command at the start of his rise in Andhra politics and once, as the PCC chief in the mid-1980s, he even had to wait for three days to get an audience with the then prime minister Rajiv Gandhi.

As Congress chief Sonia Gandhi led the party in showering glowing tributes on the man, who had made Andhra a Congress fort in the last few years, YSR's long-time associate M V Mysura Reddy recalls how the late leader had struggled to get an appointment with Rajiv Gandhi once.

"We came to Delhi to meet Rajiv to seek the Centre's aid for a railway-related project in the state. We stayed in the Andhra Pradesh Bhavan for three days, but didn't get an appointment. It was frustrating and insulting. Finally, a message was sent across that we were going to resign as there is no point in remaining in the party if a PCC president is not able to meet the PM. We were given an appointment then," he told.

Mysura Reddy, incidentally, had left Congress five years ago and joined the camp of Chandrababu Naidu, YSR's arch-rival. However, he continued to share a warm relationship with YSR and has fond memories of his long friendship, which dates back to 1978. For him, YSR's death is a personal loss, ironic though it may sound since he still holds the same Reddy responsible for his exit from the Congress.

But then that is an old story for Mysura Reddy, who along with YSR were once called the two eyes of the Congress in Andhra–the comrades-in-arms from Kadapa who fought their way up in the deeply divided and caste-ridden party structure.

"People are now talking about the padayatra he had led in the run-up to the 2004 elections. But his first padayatra was in the early 1980s. He had organised it to highlight the backwardness of

Rayalaseema region. It was the success of those early programmes that might have prompted YSR to undertake a number of mass contact drives later," he says.

For Mysura Reddy, YSR was always a rebel who had locked horns with successive Congress chief ministers and once with former PM P V Narasimha Rao as well. "But his criticisms of the Congress governments despite being a party man earned him a mass following among the youth."

The Congressman with a Mass Following and Appeal

It was about 6.30 in the evening on August 24. He broke away from addressing a gathering of bankers to have a chat on how the NREGS was doing in his State. And he was as concerned with its failures as he was pleased with its overall performance. The one point where Y.S. Rajasekhara Reddy laughed was when we came to changing attitudes to the work among the village elites. Especially the decline of the contemptuous manner in which landowners used to summon Dalit or Adivasi labourers to work. "Those old attitudes had to change," he said.

Rewind to 2004, Andhra Pradesh was seen as the one state where the Congress had no chance of making a comeback in the polls. Those were the glory days of N. Chandrababu Naidu. Something YSR was soon to demolish. The terrible summer of 2003 had seen thousands of non-state "gruel centres" trying to combat a rising tide of hunger across Telangana and Rayalaseema. Remember, there was no NREGS then (The Hindu Sunday Magazine, June 15 and 22, 2003: "Gruel Centres and the Politics of Free Lunches and Hi-Tech, Low Nutrition").

Today, in the drought, the NREGS works where gruel centres struggled. But in 2003, the phrase "Congress leadership" was a contradiction in terms in the State. Most of the State's senior Congressmen were themselves in awe of Chandrababu Naidu.

YSR thought differently. He went out on a mass contact 'padayatra' and walked through village after village tapping the rising discontent. It would be wrong to call it, as some have called it, "an undercurrent." It was a torrent. One that YSR harnessed for a pathetic, demoralised, self-doubting party that leapt in alarm if the media just said 'boo.' Going to the spot was a practice he retained even after becoming Chief Minister. If he thought he saw a problem developing, he did not wait for it to come to him. This was so even with a natural calamity. As during the 2006 floods when he was all over the place directing relief operations–while his counterpart in Maharashtra, for instance, never got his feet wet.

Years before that, when the national media were still dismissive of a spate of suicides among distressed farmers, Rajasekhara Reddy was quick to visit Bandi Lakshmamma in Anantapur. She was the wife of the first reported farm suicide victim to have caught attention in Andhra Pradesh, thanks to some exceptional reporting by a few reporters in the Telugu press. By April 2004, farmers' suicides were to be among the most decisive issues of the elections in Andhra Pradesh, both to the Lok Sabha and the Assembly.

One of the first things Rajasekhara Reddy did upon becoming Chief Minister was to appoint an enthusiastic Agriculture Minister–Raghuveera Reddy from Anantapur, the district that had perhaps suffered the worst of the crisis.

Together they tried to tackle the distress. No other State declared compensation payments to so many families affected by the suicide of their breadwinners. Andhra Pradesh set up a Commission, chaired by Professor Jayati Ghosh, to study the entire gamut of agrarian distress. The macro-policies of the State and the Centre conflicted with the thrust of the Commission's excellent report, but this was still the first such effort by any State to engage with the farm crisis.

Rajasekhara Reddy as Chief Minister was ruthless, shrewd, alert and on-the-ball. Despite a larger vision that invited big trouble down the line–like his wrong and relentless stance on Special Economic Zones–he understood his State better than his colleagues. He saw the importance of hunger in all of Andhra Pradesh and not just in the rural regions. Rajasekhara Reddy massively added to the number of Below Poverty Line family cards in the State. His 2004 victory was viewed as a "rural revolt." In 2006, he swept the urban bodies, leading the Congress to an absolute majority in 68 municipalities and grabbing the chairperson's post in 75 out of 96.

The great "USP" of the Telugu Desam Party came with NTR's promise (and delivery) of rice at Rs. 2 a kg. The Congress of that time ridiculed the measure (now firmly in place in several States) and was buried in the electoral avalanche that followed. Years after the TDP moved away from that legacy, YSR was to grab it and even project it (in factual terms quite wrongly) as a Congress idea–Indiramma's dream. In 2009, cheap rice on the Public Distribution System proved a huge boost to all those governments providing it. Andhra Pradesh gave the Congress more MPs than any other State. More than Maharashtra and Karnataka put together. Rajasekhara Reddy had stolen the clothes the TDP had discarded. Among Congress Chief Ministers, he stood out as someone who was his own man. Irascible and on a short-fuse but decisive, he rose above and held together an incoherent and faction-ridden party. As a leader he was cocky, contradictory, yet often strangely convincing.

The 2009 polls also saw him at his shrewd best. YSR was delighted when the Left opted to go with Chandrababu Naidu's TDP and not with Chiranjeevi's PRP. He was gambling on Chiranjeevi doing what Chiranjeevi did–draw away the anti-Congress vote. Rajasekhara Reddy was going by the only precedent there was–the 1978 State elections when the then "Brahmananda Reddy Congress" polled roughly what the PRP did this time, diverting the anti-Congress vote and gutting the Janata Party. That was the year YSR entered politics, and he remembered its lesson well. He ends his innings as the only Congressman in the State with a mass following and appeal, so evident in the outpouring of grief across the State.

Man for All Reasons

A decade ago when Sharad Pawar was quitting the Congress over Sonia Gandhi's foreign origin issue, he told a group of journalists, "In the Congress party, there is no place for genuine mass leaders. There is only the high command and the loyal followers."

That was 1999. Ten years later, it seems that Pawar was both right and wrong. He was right because in the Congress, the high command is ubiquitous and the Supreme Leader is unchallenged. But he was wrong that the Congress could no longer throw up a regional satrap.

Y.S. Rajasekhara Reddy was proof that it's still possible to be a virtual one-man show in state politics, and yet survive in the Congress. When YSR became chief minister in 2004, he was fighting both history and geography.

Congress chief ministers in Andhra had mastered the art of musical chairs. The previous Congress government in 1989 had seen three chief ministers in five years and the one before that, four CMs in five years (a chaotic situation that eventually saw the rise of the idea of 'Andhra pride' in the guise of N.T. Rama Rao).

Even the wily P.V. Narasimha Rao, who was able to stay as prime minister for a full five-year term as head of a minority government, could only last for 15 months in Hyderabad in the 1970s. It was almost as if it was more difficult to manage the complex caste and regional factions in Andhra than it was to control politics at the Centre.

More so in YSR's case because he came from the relatively backward region of Rayalaseema, not seen as dominant in state politics. And yet, he was able to prove the sceptics wrong by lasting the full five-year term, and, even more remarkably, by getting re-elected with an equally comprehensive mandate.

What made YSR succeed where others had failed? His critics will tell you that his political style was more akin to Gujarat's Narendra Modi than to any traditional Congress state leader. He was ruthless (witness the manner in which he crushed all political opposition to him) and anti-democratic (notice how he jailed editors and sought to financially destroy those who spoke out against him).

That YSR could get away with his authoritarian streak was due to his ability to build a firm rapport with the masses, a quality first detected during his hugely successful padyatra in 2003.

Chandrababu Naidu may have been feted by the pink papers, but he was eventually consumed by the euphoria of having been anointed the CEO of Cyberabad. YSR, on the other hand, was able to combine strong doses of populism with a delivery system that reached out to rural Andhra.

Whether it was the success of his health insurance scheme, his irrigation projects or the spread of the National Rural Employment Guarantee Scheme, he was able to convince a majority of Andhraites that he would benefit the poor with direct cash transfers, even if it meant bypassing the traditional elites of the state. In the process, he was able to overcome the caste and regional divides that had previously stunted governance.

The idea of a separate state of Telangana, for example, may have an emotional resonance, but what price statehood when there's no cash in your bank account? In that sense, YSR had the 'common man' touch, originally promoted by NTR, whose two rupee rice scheme, for example, revolutionised the trajectory of Andhra politics, creating the basis for a pro-poor programme that has since been replicated in other states. YSR did not have NTR's charisma and star appeal, but a certain down-to-earth welfarist approach to politics where he did not forget that his power was dependent on the support of the aam admi.

No surprises then that YSR was a great favourite of Sonia Gandhi, whose political philosophy is based on the core idea that the Congress's future lies in reaching out to India's poor. In fact, it would be no exaggeration to suggest that the UPA would not have been in power in 2004 and 2009 but for the remarkable success it achieved in AP. But the flip side of creating a personality cult in a political party is that when the individual disappears from the scene, the resultant vacuum is almost impossible to fill.

That will be the big challenge confronting the Congress as it comes to terms with the loss of its strongest chief minister. Will the party revert to its time-tested formula of imposing a 'weak' leader on a state in the belief that such a CM will be acceptable to all factions? Or will it acknowledge that the YSR phenomenon demands a search for another tough, empowered state leader? In resolving this dilemma, we will know if YSR was indeed the last Congress egional satrap.

He Defeated Defeat Itself'

Dr Yeduguri Sandinti Rajasekhara Reddy was perhaps the most powerful Congress Chief Minister in the country, one who had proved that he could win elections on his own merit. YSR, as he was popularly known, along with Delhi Chief Minister Sheila Dikshit, was the Congress's answer to the BJP's troika of Narendra Modi, Raman Singh and Shivraj Chouhan, who were touted by their party as models of governance just before the recent Lok Sabha polls. And this was his more enduring contribution to not just the Congress's success in 2009, but to the national imagination.

Tracing his beginnings to the ruthless, often cutthroat politics of Rayalseema–from where he was elected as an MLA four times and as an MP for four terms (he never lost an election)–YSR, who turned 60 in July, was known to be a dangerous opponent. But he was also known as someone who could turn foes into friends–political and otherwise.

To his loyalists, he was very generous, often giving unexpected rewards, as in the case of his former driver, Suryam. About 20 years ago, while YSR was still a budding politician in his native place of Kadapa, Suryam took a bullet meant for him during an attack by a rival faction. Since then, Suryam was like a family member, usually seen a few inches behind YSR throughout the day, like a shadow.

P Sabita Indra Reddy, wife of a former TDP minister who was killed by Maoists, was rewarded by YSR when the shy housewife decided to join the Congress instead of the TDP. YSR gave her a Congress ticket to contest the 2004 elections, which she won. When she was re-elected earlier this year, he made her the state's first woman home minister.

Recently, K Roja, former actress and president of the TDP women's wing who had spewed venom against the Congress and YSR during the elections, went to meet him, seeking to join the Congress. When she came out of the meeting, she said: "Although I said a lot of bad things about him, he treated me like a daughter today."

"He could win over even his most ardent detractors and foes, and that is the strength that made him such a powerful leader. He never forgot a friend or a favour and, more importantly, he repaid it in manifold," says YSR's longtime friend, K V P Ramachandra Murthy.

Combining a shrewd strategy of making his loyalists more loyal and elbowing out his rivals and detractors, YSR went on to become the most powerful Congress leader in more than 30 years in the state. "He would pick up novices and back them with all his might even in the face of dissent from within the party. They all turned out to be winners," says Congress leader Tulasi Reddy.

His grit and determination, as well as his ability to gamble politically and take risks, brought the Congress back to power in 2004, after a long gap of 13 years. Known among his supporters as the "Lion of Kadapa", it was his down-to-earth charm that led to his emergence as an extremely popular and loved leader.

It was in the scorching heat of April 2003, against the advice of some of his party leaders, that YSR started a marathon 1,450-km padayatra across the state to assess the condition of people living in backward areas. The grueling three-month walk through some of the most backward constituencies took its toll, and YSR collapsed while he was nearing Rajahmundhry. He was bedridden for nearly five days. Though a team of doctors advised him to return home and rest, YSR refused to give up the padayatra. He managed to walk along coastal Andhra, right up to Itchapuram bordering Orissa, where it ended. A year later the Congress swept to power.

"It was a gamble that paid off. Chandrababu Naidu was already in trouble due to the failure of monsoons. By concentrating only on urban areas, information technology and industry, Naidu had alienated himself from the masses. The iron was hot and YSR struck first with his padayatra and then by picking and backing winners," says a Congress leader.

The padayatra proved to be the turning point in the way YSR positioned himself and deeply influenced his politics and policies when in office. Through his schemes and proposals, he kept in touch with the masses, giving them a stake in the state's growth. His Sundays were reserved for mass contact programmes. Soon, he skillfully turned the milieu of aggressive politics he had been originally schooled in, to transform into a mass leader–putting his thundering oratorial skills and forthright manner to good use.

The People's CM

As the Leader of Opposition in the Assembly during Chandrababu Naidu's rule, YSR had often suffered political wilderness. But even as Naidu was launching Cyberabad, hosting Bill Clinton in the state capital, and being feted as CEO CM, YSR sensed an opportunity to strike back. As his official website profile puts it, YSR knew how "to defeat defeat itself." In 2000, he, along with the Left, launched a protest against the raised power tariffs, leading MLAs in a high-profile hunger strike that carried on for two weeks.

Earlier this year, the line-up against YSR was considered quite formidable–friends-turned-foes like the Left and TRS who joined hands with the TDP to form a "Mahakootami" (grand alliance), and popular filmstar Chiranjeevi who was making his political debut. But YSR confidently told several of his unbelieving and diffident party leaders in New Delhi that he would better his record of 29. And he did just that, giving the Congress its largest chunk of MPs in the country–33 out of the total 42 seats in the state.

In a party, which is not known to look kindly upon chief ministers with too much clout, YSR was an exception, having won the trust of both Congress president Sonia Gandhi and Prime Minister Manmohan Singh. He was allowed a free hand in running the state and fashioning its politics. So, despite accounting for 33 LS seats, none of the state Congress MPs, barring Jaipal Reddy, who was never seen as a threat to YSR, found place in the Union Cabinet.

Since May 2004, YSR launched over 20 schemes for the poor–health, education, minority and Dalit welfare–and made sure that the delivery mechanisms worked and benefits percolated down the chain. The Rajiv Arogyasri Rural Health Insurance scheme, which was very close to his heart, is now being replicated by the Centre in Delhi. The scheme provides for free healthcare to low income groups, including free surgeries that are performed at some of the best government and private hospitals. He also launched a well-publicised ambulance-at-your-doorstep scheme under Rajiv Arogyasri.

Then there was Abhaya Hastam, a pension scheme for women which endeared him to the 1.20 crore poor and destitute women across the state. The Indiramma low-cost housing scheme meant that even BPL families would have at least a two-room house to live in. He also re-introduced the Rs 2-per-kg rice scheme while providing free power to farmers and subsidies for buying seeds and fertilisers.

His idea of refunding fees to backward class and minority students is ensuring that fewer youths drop out of schools and colleges due to financial difficulties. Despite warnings of a cash crunch from the Finance Department and the 13th Finance

Commission, YSR embarked on a massive irrigation programme involving 61 new irrigation projects including a 600-km-long canal so that lakhs of hectares of land in remote and dry areas could be irrigated and several hundred towns and villages could get drinking water.

In effect, YSR re-defined and broad-based the idea of economic reforms, ensuring it made sense to the electorate, so much so that even the Satyam scam, which detractors claimed would hurt him, left him unscathed. He had no qualms about dramatic shifts in his politics, as and when necessary. After championing the cause of Telangana, he did a notorious "T-turn" after the polls were over.

When it came to the extreme Left, who were becoming increasingly powerful when he first assumed office in 2004, he was first open to talking to them. But when necessary, YSR was very flexible about shutting the doors on them, mounting one of the most aggressive anti-Naxal operations.

Politicians' Politician

Yeduguri Sandinti Rajasekhara Reddy was a politicians' politician. Perhaps as complete a politician as can be–aggressive in his youth, mellow in his mature avatar as chief minister, with his share of significant achievement and controversy. He combined mass appeal with an administrative acumen that made him the first Congress CM to complete a full five-year term in Andhra and then return to power, triumphant within his party and without, with a formidable record of never personally losing an electoral contest. In sum, Reddy's distinction was the thin line he astutely walked between the extremes of ivory-tower policy-making and vacuous populism. Thus YSR was seen to deliver on both economic growth and welfare, and serve as a model CM: putting an equal emphasis on industry and agriculture, stressing information and bio-technology while bequeathing to the country an eminently replication-worthy legacy in rural healthcare, largescale irrigation, housing for the poor and the tackling of the Naxalite menace. (Incidentally, the NREGS was launched at Anatapur in Andhra.) YSR's packed itinerary, with frequent flights to put his imprimatur on state projects big and small was his way of doing business.

YSR became the Congress's most powerful Andhra figure, ironically, by debunking the wishy-washy style of Congress functioning and firmly endorsing the implementation model of governing, personally keeping tabs on the performance of his MLAs and bureaucrats. On Wednesday, YSR was on his way to examine the effectiveness of state delivery mechanisms in drought-affected Rayalseema through a "mass contact" programme. He set the tone for this style of governance when, in 2003, he undertook the near-1500 km padayatra across the state that helped him dislodge the Telugu Desam Party from power the next year. Having rebuilt a written-off Congress in Andhra by himself, YSR delivered seats to the party high command, enjoying a latitude that usually eludes Congress regional stalwarts, even those as prominently "dissident" in the P.V. Narasimha Rao days as YSR–who had then been passed over for CM–was.

No politician evades blemish; the Andhra opposition compiled a famously thick dossier on YSR, while the NREGS implementation has been hardly perfect in its pilot state. But the flip side of a powerful political figure, who almost single-handedly runs a state as big as Andhra, is the vacuum his/ her absence creates. It is going to be very difficult for both the party and the state to fill YSR's place. But it is imperative that his work be carried on; in seeking YSR's successor, the Andhra Congress and the state administration must not fall apart. The Congress high command in New Delhi and the Union government must closely coordinate with Hyderabad through these difficult times.

A Mass Leader

Y. S. Rajasekhara Reddy, who grew from the faction-ridden and often violence-marked politics of Kadapa, steered his party through spectacular victories twice consecutively in the Assembly and Lok Sabha elections to emerge its undisputed leader in Andhra Pradesh.

The 60-year-old, Reddy was equally controversial as he was popular. He was a lot mellowed once he assumed reins of power, compared to the aggressive image he had acquired from his days in student Congress and later as an MLA and MP.

Dr. Reddy was impatient with the party High Command when under the late P V Narasimha Rao, Vijayabhaskara Reddy was made the chief minister in the mid-1990s but some sane counsel from the former Prime Minister softened him to bide his time.

But with Telugu Desam under Chandrababu Naidu riding high in a state where Information Technology became the buzzword and rampant farmers' suicide taking place, the Congress leader from rural Kadapa set out on a padayatra with rural transformation as his goal.

He vowed to dislodge Naidu from power in 1999 or take political sanyas but failed in that attempt. His big moment, however, came in 2004 when led the almost-written off Congress to power after a gap of ten years. Since then there was no looking back for the doctor-turned politician.

Taking over as Chief Minister in 2004 when the naxal menace was at its peak, Dr. Reddy, brought the Left-wing extremists to the negotiating table and had to take them on the plank of development when they refused to lay down arms.

He injected development in rural areas where Naxals were dominating and launched several welfare programmes and irrigation schemes in a state which had witnessed unprecedented farmer suicides before he came to power. Known for his leadership qualities, Dr. Reddy reached out to all factions of the Congress and undertook a 1,450-km padayatra in 2003 which eventually brought the party to power. Dr. Reddy also had the blessings of Sonia Gandhi, who had given him a free hand in running the government and also the 2009 election campaign.

Even on the vexed Telangana issue, both the UPA and Congress high command chose to back Dr. Reddy's line despite losing friends like Telangana Rashtra Samiti. His clout went up further when Congress wrested about seven seats in Telangana region in the by-elections in 2008.

And the Congress went alone in the 2009 elections despite the emergence of Praja Rajyam (PRP) led by popular actor Chiranjeevi solely trusting Dr. Reddy, who assured that he will bring the party back to power. It was a tough challenge for Dr. Reddy, who faced a double-barrel attack from TDP-led Grand Alliance and PRP, to storm back to power on the single agenda of development.

Dr. Reddy achieved it by touring at least 174 of the 294 Assembly constituencies in the state and axing non-performing ministers and MLAs.

On the one hand, he attracted by introducing welfare schemes like permanent housing, monthly pension and health insurance for the poor while on the other hand he was the constant target of opposition over charges of corruption, nepotism and abuse of power.

Unlike his predecessors, Dr. Reddy had little trouble within the party and enjoyed a free run for five years. In the process, he secured a firm footing in the good books of the Congress high command. Recognising his leadership qualities, the then Prime Minister and AICC president Indira Gandhi made him the chief of Andhra Pradesh Congress Committee in 1982. But Dr. Reddy quit the Congress following a split and joined the Reddy Congress in revolt against Indira Gandhi.

After the Reddy Congress was disbanded, he returned to the parent party and went on to become the PCC president again in 1997 when Telugu Desam Party was in power and his erstwhile party colleague N Chandrababu Naidu was at the helm of affairs of the state.

From 1980-1983 he was a minister holding important portfolios related to Rural Development, Medical Health and Education. He was elected to the Lok Sabha from Kadapa constituency four times and was elected to the Andhra Pradesh State Assembly six times from Pulivendula constituency. Dr. Reddy was the leader of the opposition in the State Assembly for five years.

Balanced Approach toward the Development

Dr. YSR could successfully relieve the State reeling under the economic drought situation caused by the earlier regime in the name of a disinvestment process. This posture alone speaks volumes of his way of getting things done. For the last two years, as CM of Andhra Pradesh,Dr. YSR has been successfully pushing forth the priorities of multi pronged economic strategy with a thrust on rural sector. Free power to the mute millions of the State–comprising almost 80 per cent of the State's population–that have been surviving on agriculture, testifies his commitment to his own promises. The greatest achievement of Dr. YSR, that any biographer to come could never miss to highlight, is providing a human angle to the heartless mechanism of the state. The confidence his government could induce into the marrows of the farming community makes every Telugu man proud. Today, if the Congress rule in A.P. is known as 'The Farmers' regime' all over the world, it is but for this very reason.

Another feather on Dr. YSR's cap is winning the hearts of the hardcore advocates against the Free Power Supply to the favour of farmers of our State by presenting before them an invincible brief. The Prime Minister of India Dr. Manmohan Singh recently showered the choicest encomiums on Dr. YSR for his "balanced approach toward the development of industry and agriculture in the State". It stands doubly relevant as Dr. Singh happens to be an internationally renowned economist too. It is everyone's knowledge that such a stance is rather mandatory and imperative for the accelerated growth of a dynamic and kicking economy like ours. Planners in India and abroad were at tandem in acknowledging Dr. YSR's "exceptional discretion as a policy maker" in contributing his best for the healthy growth of the key and vital sectors of our economy; namely the agriculture and the industry.

Padayatra and Sea of Popularity for YSR

The landmark achievement of Dr. Reddy, which placed him at the peak state, was his 1500 KM long Marathon Walk across the state in the blistering summer of 2003. The stellar performance of the Congress leader left the opposition awe-struck and defenseless in the general elections later. Covering his semi-bald pate with a towel and protesting his feet with Nike shoes Rajasekhara Reddy shocked his opponents with his "Walk Marathon". It also gave him a first hand insight into the problems of the farmer and also sufferings of the rural poor.

"I not only came in close contact with rural India that I belong to and love very much, but my padayatra also gave me an insight into the bureaucratic road blocks which came in the way of reaching the benefits to the common man", YSR told his associates after the walkathon of 2003. The Padayatra also helped him to consolidate his vision on the needs of the farmer and common man, and also that interim measures and adhocism would not yield expected end-results. "I firmly believed in what late Prime Minister Rajiv Gandhi had said that hardly one-tenth of a rupee spent reached the beneficiary. Hence my focus on free power and irrigation projects, land distribution and enhanced agricultural credit", says YSR.

When Dr. YSR, the then Leader of the Opposition in the Andhra Pradesh Assembly, planned to take up a padayatra in the hot summer of 2003, the friends and the foes alike tried their best to dispirit him. But it is very hard to argue with someone when he is right. It is said that the greatest challenge of life is to decide what's important and to disregard everything else. And, that's how none could stop Dr. YSR from creating history.

Even the simplest of tasks will be rated great when it is done in the right spirit. And, what about a great task done in the proper spirit? Just refer to the annals of the contemporary Andhra politics, where you find this "Empathy tour" which provided that most needed "pint of confidence" to the drought hit farming community of the State as a glorious chapter. Stretching to an extent of about 1500 K.M, from Chevella in the South Telangana to the Itchapuram in the North Andhra, this prajaprasthanam padayatra went on for 64 days. Every means of communication - the electronic and the print media alike-prominently placed "stories" covering almost every inch covered in the padayatra. Above all, every section of the society found it relevant and flooded Dr. YSR's padayatra with requests, requisitions, petitions and complaints. Everyone, inclusive of Dr. YSR, was worrying whether the "public" was aware of the fact that he was then just a leader of the Opposition and not the ruler proper. Yet, the whole thing went on all along. Eventually, these requests, requisitions, petitions and complaints formed as a firm database for Dr. YSR, the Chief Minister to efficiently act upon.

Let's back-focus on the prajaprasthanam padayatra to find out what was the reason behind this padayatra to be marked as a glorious chapter in the annals of Andhra. To state the fact, Dr. YSR was not the only politician or the first one who took up a padayatra to highlight a particular problem that was plaguing a large number of people in a particular place at a particular juncture. Padayatras were of course a part of Gandhian tradition to reflect and resound the anger of the people to reach the deaf ears of the unkind rulers. Many great soldiers of the Freedom Struggle did resort to this practice and could successfully attract the attention of the State. A parallel can be drawn between prajaprasthanam padayatra and the Raithu rakshana yatra that went along the coastal line of the state–from Itchapuram to Tada–under the leadership of a great Gandhian of his times, Late Kommareddy Satyanarayana in the third decade of the last century .

But, prajaprasthanam padayatra was entirely unique on many counts. Prajaprasthanam never had any specific agenda–an open or hidden–for that matter. As Dr. YSR, the then Opposition Leader on the floor of the Legislative Assembly was not allowed to raise his voice in favour of the suffering farmers of the state, who were resorting to the cynical suicides enmasse, he had no other go but to reach the masses face-to-face. YSR knows too well that, silent company is often more healing than empty words of advice. He didn't go there seeking a vote or begging for party funds. Instead, Dr. YSR went to every nook and corner of the state relaying the message of Empathy for the struggling sections of our State. This makes it uncomparable to any of the padayatras whatsoever. The farmers and the artisans of our State were given a raw deal by the then Government.

A drought for four consecutive years had eaten away the self-confidence of the people. And the endurance levels in the rural areas had gone to the rock bottom. What they needed most at that juncture was a kind word, a note of solace and an utterance of moral succour. Those were the very things Dr. YSR could provide to the farmers, artisans and other sections of the rural poorfolk of the state. And, for this timely gesture the history remembers him forever!

There is yet another factor–a personal one–that made the prajaprasthanam padayatra, historic. During the padayatra Dr. YSR fell seriously ill at Madhurapudi, a village close to Rajahmundry. He was terribly bitten by the hot waves of Godavari District– sending the Mercury levels upto 44 Degrees C–and was forced to be bed-ridden for about a week. Apart from the large numbers of masses that were eyewitness to his suffering, every notable head in the state was worried and concerned about the state of his health. A number of leaders from all the streams of politics flew down to Madhurapudi where Dr. YSR was being treated by a team of doctors. But none could scare the strong willed YSR in pursuing his further course. He walked down the North Coast to reach Itchapuram where he concluded the epoch making prajaprasthanam padayatra. A person's degree of self-confidence greatly determines his success, observed a wizard. After all, one cannot grow into a hero without taking a risk, people say.

3

Assembly Election 2004: YSR Reddy Voted to Power

In the Assembly election 2004, Congress got a clean win with 186 seats, followed by TDP with 45 seats, TRS with 26 seats and other parties with 37 seats altogether. One could say that it was ingenuous leadership of Dr. Reddy that helped the Congress to return to power in AP after a lapse of almost a decade and eclipse the TDP and the more than life image of its leader N Chandrababu Naidu that haunted the Congress Party. And without any opposition, Reddy was appointed Chief Minister of Andhra Pradesh.

Rajasekhara Reddy stunned the ruling party, the TDP, in the assembly and also outside with his forceful and well documented deliveries in the House. He steered the struggle against Naidu regime's power reforms without human face by bringing back anti-TDP and anti-BJP political forces together on a platform and staged an indefinite hunger strike against the government. He championed the cause of the masses and highlighted the issues of farmers, weavers, dalits, youth and women embracing the TDP regime day–in and day-out.

Andhra Pradesh: available trends 294/294			
Party	**Won**	**Lead**	**L+W**
INC+	**226**	**0**	**226**
BJP+	**49**	**0**	**49**
Others	**19**	**0**	**19**

Source: Election Commision of India

INC+							
Party	**Won**	**Lead**	**Total**	**Gain ***	**Retain**	**Total**	**Loss ***
INC	185	0	185	123	62	185	29
TRS	26	0	26	26	0	26	0
CPM	9	0	9	7	2	9	0
CPI	6	0	6	6	0	6	0
Total	**226**	**0**	**226**	**162**	**64**	**226**	**29**

Source: Election Commision of India

BJP+							
Party	**Won**	**Lead**	**Total**	**Gain ***	**Retain**	**Total**	**Loss ***
TDP	47	0	47	15	32	47	148
BJP	2	0	2	2	0	2	12
Total	49	0	49	17	32	49	160

Source: Election Commision of India

Others							
Party	**Won**	**Lead**	**Total**	**Gain***	**Retain**	**Total**	**Loss***
IND	11	0	11	10	1	11	4
AIMIM	4	0	4	0	4	4	0
JP	2	0	2	2	0	2	0
SP	1	0	1	1	0	1	0
BSP	**1**	**0**	**1**	**1**	**0**	**1**	**0**

Source: Election Commision of India

Chandrababu Naidu was an expert in downloading the lingo from the IT world and using it fashionably in statecraft to earn the image of an IT-savvy Chief Minister, even as the numbers of starvation deaths and farmers' suicides were mounting in his state under his regime. No wonder, his cyber regime just got deleted at the press of a button! Naidu escaped from the PWG's claymore mines but the bombshell dropped by the electorate finished him off politically.

Chandrababu Naidu went in for early elections hoping to harvest the sympathy over the PWG's assassination attempt against him and also hoping that the Vajpayee factor would click in the Lok Sabha polls and the decision badly boomeranged on him. Naidu would have been thrown out in the last elections itself. But his promise of free gas ovens for the rural poor under his populist Deepam scheme somehow enabled him to ride back to power. The rural poor who never got the gas ovens have taken sweet revenge this time.

It is a clear verdict against the World Bank-inspired reform process set in motion by the Chandrababu government. The English media is clueless about the severe drubbing received by their darling CM. In particular, the pink papers are bemoaning his defeat. "The fisc is likely to come under tremendous pressure (due to free supply of power to the farmers). Labour reform will have to wait a bit more. Fresh hikes in FDI will become difficult", lamented the Economic Times (15 May, 2004). The Financial Times grumbled that the Congress party's populist promise to extend free power to the state's agricultural sector could increase the subsidy tab by over 30 per cent from Rs. 1,303.27 crore to Rs 1,712.44 crore–an increase of over Rs 400 crore–for 2004-05 (FT, 12 May, 2004). "Naidu's defeat is a victory for democracy but defeat for development", commented another business paper.

It is a humiliating defeat for the ruling TDP, with 28 out of the 36 Ministers who contested getting defeated and the party totally routed in Khammam, Nizamabad, Nellore and Medak districts and winning only one seat each in Nalgonda, Mahbubnagar and Kurnool districts. The Congress led alliance that included left parties and Telengana Rashtra Samiti (TRS) bagged 226 seats out of 294 in the state. The TDP alliance managed to bag only 49 seats and while its ally, the BJP, has won in just two constituencies and others bagged 19 seats.

Contrary to the image projected by the English media, Andhra Pradesh was the worst performing state in South India. Its growth of real income, or Gross Domestic Product, has been only around 5 per cent per annum since 1995. This was the lowest among all the southern states and less than the all-India average of 8%. Similarly, employment growth in AP was lower than the national average over the period between 1993 and 2000. In terms of literacy and school enrolment, Andhra Pradesh is well below the national average and ranks among the worst States in India. School dropout rates are among the highest in India. The infant mortality rate is higher than the national average, and has shown an increase in recent years. Under Naidu, Andhra Pradesh has become a highly indebted state with loans to the tune of Rs.40,000 crore. He went scrounging for funds from international institutions and borrowed heavily from the World Bank, only to spend the money to improve the infrastructure in Hyderabad in favour of Indian and foreign monopolies. During his last days the state got caught in a debt trap and he was borrowing only to pay interest for the accumulated debt.

Chandrababu Naidu was among the first chief ministers in India to carry out the World Bank-prescribed electricity reforms. He steeply hiked the power rates. CPI (ML) Liberation, CPI, CPI(M) and six other left parties jointly conducted a massive agitation and Chandrababu's government fired on the agitators, killing a few.

There were severe droughts in 2002-03 and 2003-04 in Andhra Pradesh. In Anantapur district there were mass starvation deaths and indebted farmers were committing suicides in large numbers. Chandrababu Naidu did not do anything to ameliorate the condition of the farmers. When CPI (ML) Liberation organised a road blockade on the busy National Highway-5, running between Calcutta and Chennai, Naidu's police brutally beat up many women and seriously injured them. But it evoked a tremendous response among the drought-affected farmers.

The women voters in Andhra Pradesh rejected Chandrababu's regime completely. The reason is not difficult to seek. Chandrababu formed more than 2 lakh DWACRA (Development of Women and Children in Rural Areas) groups in the state and promised to extend Rs.10,000 revolving fund to each of them. He also promised to set up a Mahila Bank with a paid-up capital of Rs.2,000 crore. With these promises he collected several hundred crores from women as savings but not even one per cent of the groups were extended loans. In fact, he collected more from the women than what he gave them. He received poetic justice at their hands during elections.

The Left parties have won 16 constituencies. Though they conducted an independent mass movement against the TDP regime, unfortunately the CPI and CPI (M) aligned with the Congress and won these seats. It is not that the Congress alliance was indispensable for the Left. The CPI (M) won the Khammam Lok Sabha seat contesting independently fighting against the Congress since Congress refused to leave any Lok Sabha seat to the CPI (M). The CPI and CPI (M) should have tried the Khammam model in the assembly elections also and fought independently with the support of other left formations and that would have enabled the Left to emerge as a powerful independent political force in the state. The CPI (ML) New Democracy has won its traditional seat Illendu in Khammam district through independent contest. CPI (ML) Liberation polled 4,619 votes in Pratipadu, 4.013 in Polavaram, 2,374 in Tuni, 1,816 in Jaggampeta, 1,623 in Paykaraopeta, 1,267 in Pithapuram, 1,201 in Sompeta and 1,040 in Sampara, 925 in Avanigadda and 725 in Tiruvuru.

BJP Paid for its Miserable Understanding of the Public Pulse

The Bharatiya Janata Party (BJP) paid for its miserable understanding of the public pulse in Andhra Pradesh. Not only did it draw a nought in the Lok Sabha elections from the state, its poor performance here spoilt its chances of forming the next government at the Centre. In the last Lok Sabha, BJP represented eight constituencies from the state, while its ally Telugu Desam Party (TDP) represented 31 seats out of the total 42 Lok Sabha seats.

The leadership of Atal Bihari Vajpayee as a poll plank worked wonders in the last general elections. In the 1999 elections, the popularity of Vajpayee rode high following the Kargil conflict and the testing of the nuclear bomb, fetching about 18 per cent votes for BJP in the 1999 elections in the state.

At present, the vote share has nose-dived to less than three per cent. This time round the Congress alone has won 29 seats and its allies have won another seven, which has strongly changed the arithmetic at the Centre.

MIM has retained its lone Hyderabad constituency. As the BJP state leaders had widely proclaimed that they would sail or sink with TDP, they did the latter by tying themselves tightly to the TDP, which was losing its buoyancy. In fact, the BJP has lost its base in its traditional strongholds by relinquishing the Telangana statehood demand.

The BJP leadership's decision to go in for early polls was largely influenced by Naidu's early dissolution of the Assembly. In fact, the decision to go in for early elections was taken by BJP in Hyderabad.

Once known for his opposition to simultaneous Lok Sabha and Assembly elections for fear that it would ruin the prospects of TDP, Naidu later took a diametrically opposite view when he badly needed to cash in on Vajpayee's image to come back to power. In fact, it was the TDP that gained from its alliance with the BJP in earlier elections. Although it polled lesser number of votes than the Congress in the 1999 elections, it could still retain power largely because of the strong performance of the BJP.

Even in the Lok Sabha elections, the BJP-TDP combine wrested 39 out of the 42 constituencies because of the simultaneous Lok Sabha and Assembly elections in 1999. This time round when the state BJP depended mainly on the strength of its major partner for improving its position, it was the TDP, which pinned hopes on the 'feel good factor' played up by the BJP.

With the TDP's support being crucial for the survival of the National Democratic Alliance (NDA), the state BJP leaders had to forego the long-term interests of the party and acceded to the whims of Telugu Desam. This has proved to be the BJP's greatest undoing and the very survival of the party in Andhra Pradesh is threatened.

The BJP state leaders had for long been used to being "treated well by Chandrababu Naidu for the remaining voiceless friends". Naidu at times showed intolerance to any kind of criticism from the ally. Being a local man, Venkaiah Naidu, at the party's helm of affairs, has also proved to be a liability for the state BJP.

His opinions were seen to be influenced by the Telugu Desam and a particular social grouping of the affluent coastal Andhra region. The state BJP leaders lost touch with the ground realities, which resulted in their total rout in the current elections.

It could get only two seats in the Assembly elections. It appears, the BJP national leaders, some of them known for their political acumen, too believed in the magical powers of Chandrababu Naidu.

Despite several indications of a deepening crises in the agriculture sector and public resentment, they never tried to advise Naidu to shift his priorities. The voters of Andhra Pradesh seemed to have expressed their strong disapproval over this, by distancing themselves from both the parties together.

Arithmetic and Anti-incumbency Knocked Naidu Out

The simultaneous election in Andhra Pradesh became a referendum on Chandrababu Naidu's nine-year rule. While he saw an "anti-opposition wind" blowing in the State, the verdict delivered a double blow to the TDP-BJP alliance. Everything seems to have gone against him. The sympathy factor did not work; women did not vote in large numbers for him as he expected; farmers, backward classes and the youth sided with the Congress more than the TDP.

Party	Seats won	Net gain	Vote%	Change from99
TDP	47	-133	37.33	-6.54
BJP	2	-10	2.82	-0.85
Congress	185	94	38.25	-2.36
TRS	26	26	6.36	6.36
CPI(M)	9	7	1.38	-0.32
CPI	6	6	1.4	0.85

Source: National Informatics Centre-Assembly Elections 2004

For the first time, two alliances fought against each other in the elections making it the most intensely contested elections in a polarised situation. The Congress followed the alliance tactics adopted by the TDP from the beginning. It forged an alliance with the Left parties in the State. The alliance with the newly formed sub-regional party, Telangana Rashra Samiti, paid huge dividends in the Telangana region. It also performed much better in the coastal region, contrary to speculation that its alliance with the separatist TRS would invite the wrath of the people of the coastal region. In this Lok Sabha election, the Congress polled 41.5 per cent votes, which is less than the 42.8 per cent votes that it got in the 1999 Lok Sabha elections. But it won 29 seats this time, whereas it could win only five seats earlier. The alliance generated a momentum in favour of the Congress, far more than what it could have achieved had it gone alone. The Congress alliance got 50.6 per cent of the votes winning 36 seats. While the TDP and the BJP hoped to repeat their 1999 performance through continuing their alliance, they fared poorly by polling the same percentage of votes as the Congress did, and got only five seats. The BJP could not get even a single seat. It is a total reversal of the 1999 verdict.

While we can attribute the Congress' success to the alliance effect, we need to explain the factors that led to the loss of eight percentage points for the TDP-BJP combine. First, not many people believed in the claim the TDP made about development. The most striking is the people's dissatisfaction about shrinking employment opportunities and irrigation water. As many as 52 per cent of the voters felt that the employment opportunities had gone down under the TDP Government, while 41 per cent thought the irrigation supply had deteriorated. Two-thirds of people felt that the economic policies of the TDP Government either benefited the rich or not benefited any one. Similarly, half the voters felt that whatever development did happen took place in Hyderabad, while the rest of the State lagged behind.

Notwithstanding Mr. Naidu's image outside the State, it seems that the leadership factor did not work for the TDP. Mr. Naidu is known for his extraordinary skills in managing party and factions within the party. But a leader is judged not by his capacity for backroom management. There is a huge credibility deficiency for Mr. Naidu as a popular leader. The survey found that Congress leader Rajasekhara Reddy is rated much higher than Mr. Naidu in this respect. It is rare for a sitting CM to be beaten in popularity rating by a challenger who had never occupied the position.

The survey data shows that about one-fifth of voters who had voted for the TDP-BJP alliance in the 1999 elections had switched to the Congress-led alliance this time. Dissatisfaction with the NDA Government, and a feeling that the their financial condition has worsened, contributed to this vote change. The image the TDP acquired during N.T. Rama Rao's rule as pro-women, pro-farmer, pro-backward classes and pro-poor party has undergone a change in recent years. The change in image has been reflected in the change in social profile of the party, as the TDP-BJP combine fared badly among these social groups.

A significant proportion of the poor have supported the Congress this time. Despite the fact that Mr. Naidu's Government pursued neo-liberal economic policies since 1996, a major portion of the poorer classes voted for the TDP in the 1999 elections. The allegation levelled by the Congress and the Left parties that Mr. Naidu was acting at the dictates of the World Bank, and that the loans from abroad were used to enrich party leaders at the local level, seems to have stuck. His claim of trying to balance development (economic reforms) and welfare did not impress many. Unlike Rama Rao, Mr. Naidu is not a mass mobiliser, nor could he use pro-poor rhetoric. Unlike in 1999 he could not reel out welfare schemes on the eve of elections, which were thought to have fetched him votes then. In the implementation of welfare programmes, Mr. Naidu only sounded apologetic.

The discontent among farmers that agriculture had been neglected was widespread. This was due to poor irrigation facilities, lack of remunerative prices, inadequate market facilities, and the like, coupled with the persistent efforts of the Congress leaders to highlight them. People blamed the government for all these problems, although the TDP tried to make the point that it was due to factors beyond its control. The suicides of farmers mocked the TDP in its face. On the other hand, the Congress' promise of free power for cultivation attracted the farmers to it. Nearly 70 per cent respondents covered in the survey said that power should be supplied free. The TDP leadership hoped that the farmers, notwithstanding the discontent, would finally vote for it. This did not happen.

Thirdly, the TDP leadership banked too much on the women's vote. It hoped that women who are involved in the large number of women self-help groups (estimated to be about 4.5 lakh) would vote in their favour. About one-fifth of the TDP candidates in the Vidhan Sabha elections were women. Mr. Naidu wrote personal letters to the women in self-help groups for electoral support. Even when the exit polls predicted a rout of the TDP-BJP, Mr. Naidu was asserting that the alliance would win, because it had a lead of 10 percentage points among women. The TDP had not only lost the edge it had in 1999 elections, but it actually did worse among women voters. While the Congress alliance led the TDP-BJP by 5 percentage points among men, the lead for Congress alliance went up to 13 percentage points among women.

Fourthly, the vote the TDP received among the backward classes has also declined considerably. The strength of the TDP lies mainly in getting a large chunk of the peasant OBC vote. In 1999 it was almost double that of the Congress. In fact, one of the reasons given for the rise of the TDP to power in early 1980s was the overwhelming support from the OBCs. The TDP-BJP combine fielded 15 more BC candidates than the Congress alliance in the Assembly elections, and three more than its rival alliance in the Lok Sabha elections. But this too did not work.

Finally, the youth also voted against the TDP in large numbers than in the 1999 elections. Resentment against the TDP Government has increased over the years, mostly centred on unemployment. While 57 per cent of the youth voted for the Congress alliance, only 38 per cent voted for the TDP alliance. The TDP could not expect to win an election when it lost votes across all these social categories. Thus, it is a combination of alliance effect and the swing factor that saw a triumphant return of the Congress after a gap of almost a decade.

4

Assembly Election 2009: Reddy's Magic Worked Again

Chief Minister Y.S. Rajasekhara Reddy's magic worked once again as the Congress retained power in Andhra Pradesh with a comfortable majority. Facing a united opposition alliance and the Praja Rajyam Party (PRP) of superstar Chiranjeevi, YSR emerged victorious and achieved the distinction of being the only Congress leader after 1982 to lead the party to a second consecutive term.

Three days after becoming the first chief minister in the state's history to complete a full five years in office, YSR surprised all by leading the party to power despite the glamour of Chiranjeevi and free television and cash transfer scheme promises of the main opposition Telugu Desam Party (TDP).

With the party crossing the magic figure of 148 on its own, it does not need any party's support to form the government again. The Congress bagged 157 seats as results of all 294 assembly seats were announced.

YSR termed the results the "people's victory" and vowed to continue welfare and development schemes, especially construction of irrigation projects. The newly-elected legislators of the Congress will met on May 19 to elect YSR as the leader. He took oath as the chief minister for the second time on May 20.

TDP-led four-party grand alliance won 106 seats. Improving its position, TDP won 91 seats while Telangana Rashtra Samiti

(TRS) returned a disastrous performance winning only 10 seats. The Communist Party of India and the Communist Party of India-Marxist, the other constituents of the alliance, together won five seats.

PRP, which made its electoral debut, bagged 18 seats, far below its expectations. Majlis-e-Ittehadul Muslimeen (MIM) got seven seats and the Bharatiya Janata Party (BJP) two seats. Others, including independents, won four seats.

Despite the defeat of nearly a dozen ministers, state Congress chief D. Srinivas and speaker K.R. Suresh Reddy, YSR proved that there was no anti-incumbency factor against the government.

Unlike the TDP, which promised free color television and cash doles for the poor, the Congress sought votes on the basis of welfare and development works it undertook during the last five years.

YSR, who led the party to a landslide win in 2004 ending nearly a decade long rule of the TDP, had promised to continue free electricity to farmers, the ambitious 'Jalayagnam' or building of irrigation projects, Rajiv Arogyasri or the community health insurance scheme, housing for poor, old age and widow pension, scholarships and fee reimbursement to students belonging to weaker sections and rice at Rs.2 a kg.

The initial trends indicated that the state was heading for its first-ever hung assembly but the ruling party improved its position as the counting progressed. The TDP-led alliance has performed far below its expectations. The TDP, which had lost power to Congress in 2004 polls, had hoped to return to power with an alliance with the TRS and the two Left parties.

TRS, which had contested 2004 polls in alliance with Congress, had won 26 seats. The two Left parties had together bagged 13 seats. TDP, however, improved its position to 91 from the 45 seats it won in the previous election. In the 2004 elections, Congress had bagged 185 assembly seats on its own. Its allies, including the TRS, CPI and CPI-M had won 40 seats.

Andhra Pradesh Assembly Elections Results 2009 Information Available:-294/294	
Party	Won
INC	158
TDP	105
PRP	18
Others	13

The Congress retained power in Andhra Pradesh and improved its tally of Lok Sabha seats from the southern state, fighting off a spirited challenge from a so-called Grand Alliance of opposition parties and aided by the division of anti-Congress votes by movie star Chiranjeevi's Praja Rajyam Party, or PRP.

The ruling Congress, which also had to contend with the anti-incumbency factor, increased its Lok Sabha seats from Andhra Pradesh to 33 from the 29 it won in the last general election. Andhra Pradesh has 42 Lok Sabha seats. In the assembly elections, unlike in 2004 when it won 185 seats, the Congress secured a lower tally of 157, but still sufficient to form a government on its own. The number required for a simple majority in the 294-member assembly is 148.

Unlike in 2004, the Congress fought elections on its own this time, as former allies Telangana Rashtra Samithi (TRS) and Left parties deserted it and joined the Grand Alliance led by Telugu Desam Party.

Chief minister Y.S. Rajasekhara Reddy credited the party's success to Prime Minister Manmohan Singh and Congress president Sonia Gandhi. "I find no words to express my gratitude to you for guiding and leading us in these elections and also ensuring continuance of the Congress party in power, on its own, in Andhra Pradesh," Reddy said in letters to Singh and Gandhi.

The Congress, which political observers predicted would lose badly in the Telangana region–owing to its ambiguous stand on the issue of separate statehood for the region–did surprisingly well. It won 50 assembly seats out of 119 and 12 Lok Sabha seats out of 17 from Telangana.

"There was a clear anti-incumbency factor in the State, but the split in opposition votes helped Congress to come back to power," said political analyst C. Narasimha Rao. "The votes of urban middle-class against the government were also split by Lok Satta party. Seat sharing by TDP's allies in the Grand Alliance–TRS, CPI and CPM–where they did not enjoy a strong base also helped the fortunes of Congress."

The leaders of key parties in the state who won their seats included chief minister Reddy from Pulivendula, TDP leader N. Chandrababu Naidu from Kuppam, TRS leader K. Chandrasekhara Rao from Mahabubnagar, Chiranjeevi from Tirupati and Jayaprakash Narayan of the Lok Satta party from Kukatpalli. Several other leaders lost. Union minister for women and child welfare Renuka Chowdhary was defeated from Khammam.

A number of ministers in the state–Mohammed Ali Shabbir, N. Rajya Laxmi, T. Jeevan Reddy, Ratnakar Rao, Mohammed Fareeduddin, and Pinnamaneni Venkateshwara Rao, Mandali Budda Prasad, Sambhani Chandrasekhar, G. Vinod, Redya Nayak, Vanama Venkateswar Rao, Chinna Reddy and Chenga Reddy–also lost.

Chiranjeevi, who contested two Assembly seats, won from Tirupati by a margin of 10,000 votes, but surprisingly lost by over 20,000 votes from Palakol, from where he hails. His brother-in-law and PRP general secretary Allu Aravind was defeated in the Anakapalli parliamentary constituency. Another senior PRP leader, T. Devender Goud, who merged his Nava Telangana Party with PRP, lost election from both Malkajigiri Lok Sabha constituency and Ibrahimpatnam assembly seat.

Chiranjeevi had hoped to emerge as a kingmaker in the state in the event of a hung assembly. Praja Rajyam contested 282 assembly and 41 parliamentary seats. "Chiranjeevi's PRP lacked political direction, lost an historical opportunity and ended up as a spoilsport for the fortunes of Grand Alliance led by TDP in the state and helped Congress improve its tally in the Parliament polls as well," said K. Nageshwar, a political analyst and member of the Andhra Pradesh legislative council.

Despite the disappointing performance, PRP will continue to play a key role in state politics and strive to strengthen its position over a period of time, said Shravan Kumar, general secretary of the PRP's youth wing. "We seemed to have failed in effectively taking to the masses key points of our philosophy and ideology," he conceded.

Unlike the main opposition TDP, which promised free colour television and cash doles to the poor, the Congress party sought vote on the welfare and development works taken by it during last five years.

YSR, who led the party to a landslide win in 2004 ending nearly a decade long rule of the TDP, had promised to continue free electricity to farmers, the ambitious "Jalayagnam" or building of irrigation projects, "Rajiv Arogyasri" or the community health insurance scheme, housing for poor, old age and widow pensions, scholarships and fee reimbursement to students belonging to weaker sections and Rs 2 a kg rice.

The TDP-led alliance has performed far below its expectations. The TDP, which had lost power to Congress in 2004 polls, had hoped to return to power with an alliance with the TRS and the two left parties. The TRS, which had contested 2004 polls in alliance with Congress, had won 26 seats. The two left parties had together bagged 13 seats.

The TDP, however, improved its position as it had bagged only 45 seats in the last elections. In the 2004 elections, Congress had bagged 185 assembly seats on its own. Its allies, including the TRS, CPI and CPI-M, had won 40 seats.

Riding on Pro-poor and Populist Schemes

Riding on pro-poor and populist schemes, Y S Rajasekhara Reddy led the Congress to a second consecutive win in Andhra. Belying its own expectations and amidst predictions of a hung Assembly, the Congress rode back to power on the strength of its populist schemes, particularly the Rs 2 per kg rice, free power to farm sector, and Rajiv Arogya Shree free health care programme for the poor. The single most important factor that aided the Congress appears to be the half-a-dozen schemes implemented by the Government in the last five years. The party swept the Rayalaseema region and retained its hold over coastal Andhra.

The TDP, which was reduced to 47 seats in 2004 election, regained a lot of lost ground but could not break the Congress's surge. There were doubts in the Congress camp that it may lose its share of votes to the PRP in the nine districts of coastal Andhra. However, against all expectations, the Congress won 68 of the 124 seats in these districts. The party swept the four districts of Rayalaseema winning 32 of the 52 seats. In Telangana, the Congress won 57 of the 119 seats in 10 districts. The PRP failed to make any impact in East Godavari (four seats), West Godavari (one seat), Krishna (0), and Srikakulam (0) districts where it was expected to consolidate itself.

The glamourous PRP with its promise of social justice and empowerment to weaker sections, and the TDP's cash transfer scheme and promise of free television sets failed to attract voters.

As the Telangana sentiment failed to fire this time, the TRS performed dismally in Telangana where it contested 47 seats but won only 10 seats falling way short of its 2004 tally of 26.

The TDP individually won 42 of the 64 seats it contested in Telangana while allotting 45 seats to TRS and 10 seats to Left parties. Both the TRS and Left parties performed dismally, which scuttled the chances of the Grand Alliance.

The Congress fell short of its 2004 tally of 185 seats, as some heavyweights and ministers lost the election. Andhra Pradesh Congress Committee president D Srinivas, Speaker Suresh Reddy, minister Mohammed Ali Shabbir, Jeevan Reddy, Mohammed Fareeduddin, P Venkateshwara Rao, N Rajyalakshmi, wife of former CM N Janardhan Reddy, lost. Actress Roja of the TDP lost from Chandragiri.

YSR won from Pulivendala with a majority of 1,03,556 votes while TDP chief N Chandrababu Naidu won from Kuppam with a margin of 89,952 votes. Chiranjeevi won from Tirupati with a margin of 56,309, but lost from Palacole.

Locked in a triangular contest with the TDP–forming a strong opposition under the 'Maha Kutami' with the TRS and Left–and a charged-up PRP, YSR created a record by becoming the only Congress leader in the state to lead the party to a second consecutive term since 1982. A jubilant YSR said it was the party's pro-poor schemes that held it in good stead.

Reddy Sworn in as the Chief Minister for the Second Term

Powering the Congress to a spectacular win in the assembly and Lok Sabha elections Andhra Pradesh, Y S Rajasekhara Reddy was sworn in as the Chief Minister for a second consecutive term.

The only Congress chief minister of Andhra Pradesh to complete a full five-year term and also retain it, Reddy took charge of the state in 2004 at a difficult time for the party which had been out of power in the state for ten years. It was a tough challenge for Reddy, but he had always thrived in difficult times.

After graduating in medicine and practising for a while, Reddy, groomed by a family deeply involved ion public service, began his political career with Congress in mid-1970s.

Having recognised his leadership qualities, the then Prime Minister and AICC president Indira Gandhi made him the chief of Andhra Pradesh Congress Committee way back in 1982.

But Reddy quit Congress following a split and joined Reddy Congress in revolt against Indira Gandhi. After the Reddy Congress was disbanded, he returned to the parent party and went on to become the PCC president again in 1997 when Telugu Desam Party was going strong and his erstwhile party colleague N Chandrababu Naidu was calling the shots in the state.

Reddy vowed to dislodge Naidu from power in 1999 or take political 'sanyas' but failed in his attempt. However, his big moment came in 2004 when he spearheaded the almost written-off Congress to victory.

A Congress government was formed in the state after a gap of 10 years. It was widely acknowledged in Congress that it was Reddy's 1450-km padayatra (foot march) in 2003 that helped the party regain power and after the poll in 2004, he was the automatic choice of the high command for the Chief Minister's post.

Reddy made his maiden entry into the Andhra Pradesh Assembly in 1978 from his home town Pulivendula. Having represented the constituency in 1983, 1985 and 1989, he was elected to the Lok Sabha for the first time in 1991 from Kadapa and consecutively thereafter till 1998.

Reddy's stint as Chief Minister was as much controversial as popular. On the one hand, he attracted the people by introducing many populist schemes like permanent housing, monthly pensions and health insurance. On the other hand, he was targeted by the opposition over alleged corruption, nepotism and abuse of power. Unlike his predecessors, Reddy had little trouble within the party and enjoyed a free run for five years. In the process, he also cemented his place in the good books of the Congress high command.

Even on the contentious Telangana issue, the Congress high command chose to back Reddy's line despite losing political friends like Telangana Rashtra Samiti and Communist Party of India.

His clout went up further when Congress wrested about seven seats in Telangana region in the bye-elections in 2008. And, it was only on his assurance that Congress decided to venture into 2009 elections without any ally even as opposition parties joined hands and a new party like the Praja Rajyam emerged.

In the end, however, Rajasekara Reddy had the last laugh steering the party to a comfortable win the state. In his second innings, Reddy holds out the promise of giving a major thrust to information technology, biotechnology, industrial and agricultural production greater public-private partnership.

5

Development Policies and Programmes

In his endeavour to ensure the well-being of the aam aadmi, YSR Reddy surpassed his predecessor N Chandrababu Naidu, who developed IT for industrialisation, while YSR leveraged IT to ensure reach of the programmes to the beneficiaries.

YSR was known for his passion to promote irrigation through his flagship programme Jalayagnam, under which he built 26 major irrigation projects and six medium irrigation projects with an estimated investment of Rs 56,000 crore. He used to monitor the project routinely, officials said.

Another flagship programme of the deceased CM was the Indiraamma scheme to provide basic amenities to 1.82 crore rural and 45 lakh poor urban population. In the field of NREGA, Andhra Pradesh achieved an amazing 94 per cent efficiency against states like Jharkhand (whose efficiency is a mere 26 per cent) through intensive monitoring and leveraging IT designed by the Tata Consultancy Services for zeroing in on the beneficiaries. Concerned that the poor populace was unable to access proper healthcare, YSR launched the Rajiv Arogyasri wherein those Below Poverty Line were given cashless health insurance cards. About two lakh families were given such cards against the national target of 30,000 BPL families being given this healthcare through the Rashtriya Swasthya Vima Yojana.

Among his other social sector schemes was the Indira Prabha scheme which was designed to ensure effective cultivation. Jawahar Knowledge Centres were set up in every district to impart industry grade (soft) skills to female engineering students. Praja Patham was launched to ensure visits of all mandal level officers, along with concerned legislator, to all panchayats.

A Raithu Bidda

Basing on his personal interaction with the old and the aged people of the rural areas during the Prajaprasthanam Padayatra, Dr.YSR enhanced Old age pensions for the needy. This is a rare stance found in the age of political consumerism where the leaders bury their past experience as soon as they get elected to plum positions. Distributing Government lands admeasuring morethan 300000 acres to landless poor is another welfare measure that stands as a sound proof of the humane face of Dr.YSR's Ministry. A conscientious congressman, Dr.YSR has won the accolades from his friends and foes alike as a warm blooded and cool-headed man of masses. Honesty is not a virtue that was cultivated by him for years; it is rather his second nature. The way in which Dr. YSR stood loyal to his election manifesto stands as a testimony for this statement. Of late Dr. YSR, the fresh 'Role Model' in demand, evolved himself into national proportions if not international.

Harithandhra Pradesh

Rejuvenation of Agriculture is gigantic task, and the state government is determined to do it, and succeed. What Rajasekhara Reddy initiated in the first minute of his tenure as Chief Minister of the State, raised new hopes and aspirations in the entire rural community of farmers,agricultural labor and the rural unemployed. The state government waived arrears of power bills relating to agricultural consumption to the tune of Rs.1192 crore. Free power to farmers was introduced as a radical measure, first ever after the formation of the State. The measure was heckled at, and criticized as impractical and overzealous.

Now there are about 24 lakh agricultural pump sets are under power consumption in the state, out of which 95% comes under free-power category was in dire straits, with distress and frustration prevailing both in urban and rural areas, among the toiling masses and the educated youth. Ever since Dr. Y.S. Rajasekhara Reddy took over as Chief Minister, the state was being given a new face-lift with a proactive trend in its pro-active, pro-poor and profarmer as well as investor-friendly and rural oriented polices. Dr. Reddy expressed his deep anguish and grief at the desperate suicides being committed by indebted farmers in the state, though the contribution of Agriculture to the Economy of the state is about 70%. To put an end to this senseless suicide activity immediately, the state government declared moratorium on repayment of loans taken by farmers from private moneylenders for a period of 2 years. The state government has announced a Special Package of Relief & Rehabilitation for the distressed farmers, providing succour and financial relief for them. "Rajiv Gandhi Grameena Vidyudeekarana Yojana"(RGGVY) was launched at an estimated cost of Rs.1209.70 core. The scheme is envisaged to streamline and strengthen T&D system with a strong network of substations, distribution transformers and line, and thereby complete the electrification of 9283 habitations within 2 years and 45,28,025 households within 3 years in the state. The government waived collections of stamp duty in respect of crop loans to farmers. The Government is putting forth all out efforts to inculcate and spread awareness among the farmers about the latest technologies in farm cultivation by way of conducting Rythu Sadassu, Rythu Chaitanya Yatras, Polam Badi, Seed Village, Rythu Bandhu etc., and help farmers get high yield and more income at low production cost. The Government has taken up several measures to strengthen market yards and remove intervention of middlemen in purchase-and-sale process and see that remunerative price is made available to the farmers produce, particularly in case of groundnut, maize, cotton etc. The government is widely popularizing "SRI" Type of paddy cultivation and striving to bring about among the farmers about this method through a programme called "SRI Vari- Mee Inta Siri".

Aimed at economic empowerment of farmers and ensuring increased income to the farmers by way of encouraging them in ancillary sectors such as Poultry, Animal Husbandry, Fisheries, Sericulture, Water conservation etc. the State government has setup " Agricultural Technology Mission" (ATM) with effect from 15th January 2006. Now, A.P. stands No.1 in the country with highest number of agricultural pumpsets of about 23.78 lakh surpassing Maharashtra (about 22 lakh). With the addition of 1.5 lakh connections to pumpsets, the state is envisaged to cross 25-lakh mark, thus the state registering 43.63 per cent of total agricultural connections in South India. Under Ryhu Bandhu, Rs.35.88 crore was disbursed as advance to the farmers last year. One lakh more new Rythu Mitra groups would be formed, and 10.25 lakh fresh loans would be extended under credit for those who have not availed this facility so far. Registration fee and stamp duty were exempted for loans up to Rs.1 lakh to small/marginal farmers. A new state seed regulation Bill was instroduced for enhanced penalty to erring dealers of spurious seed and adequate compensation to victimized farmers. Agri-credit to farmers was increased to Rs.7,010 crore during Khariff as against Rs.5,105 crore the previous year. An alternative marketing network for horticulture produce costing about Rs.100 crore was entered into with MOU with NDDB to cut down post-harvest losses and ensure remunerative prices to farmers

Jala Yagnam

While there is abundant water of about 2745 TMC available for the state, only about 1700 M.W. of water is under utilization in the state, thus giving way to huge quantum of water to go waste into the ocean. About 4000 TMC has been going out waste following heavy rains and floods. To utilize as much of water as possible by construction of river projects and bring millions of acres of lands under cultivation in Krishna-Godavari basin. The State Government has initiated a series of 26 important irrigation projects and 4 major projects under Jayalagnam programme at huge expenditure of rs.46,000 crore, which are envisaged to bring Ten Million acres of lands under cultivation, including stabilization of 3.5 million acres of existing ayacut apart from providing drinking water to 12 million people in towns and villages across the irrigation canals and generating 2700 M.W. of Power.It is planned to complete eight of these projects within 2 years, thus bringing 16.58 lakh acres aunder cultivation.These are Vamsadhara Stage-2 Phase-1, Tatipudi Lift. Pushkaram Lift, Telugu Ganga, Somasila, Chokkarao Lift Irrigation Project (Godavari Lift), Alisagar Lift, Gupta Lift. It is programmed to complete 18 projects within 5 years and provide irrigated water to a fresh ayacut of 5 million acres. Projects like Sripadasagar (Yellampalli), Chokkarao Project Stage-2 (Godavari Lift), Rajiv Sagar Lift (Dummugudem), Link Canal from Nagarjuna Sagar Project to its Reservoir, and Indira Sagar (Polavaram) are considered to be milestones in the history of State Irrigation. State Government is determined to complete modernization of Pulivendula Branch Canal and Muylavaram Projects as well as Lendi Project with 2 years. Linking of Godavari and Krishna by constructing Indira Sagar Project and Rajiv Sagar project across River Godavari would become a landmark achievement in the entire country, thus paving way to new era in water utility. By inaugurating the Janjhavati irrigation (Rubber Dam) project in Vizianagaram district, first of its kind tobe built with Austrian Technology, during the last week of December 2005, the State Government proved that it is a performing government, giving priority to farmer's welfare. The State Government has sanctioned execution of 110 lift irrigation schemes to create an additional ayacut of 1.62 lakh acres. During 2004-05,60 LI schemes were commissioned creating a potential of 43000 acres, besides revival of 160 LI schemes with an ayacut of 80000 acres.

Rs.5200 crore Master Plan of huge number of minor irrigation schemes is being implemented for creating an additional ayacut of 1.5 million acres, and stabilization of the existing ayacut of 5 lakh acres. The budgetary allocation to Irrigation was raised from Rs.1840 crore in 2003-04 to Rs.10,400 (40% of the State's own revenue) for irrigation sector during 2005-06. An amount of Rs.1200 crore is being spent by the state government under A.P. Micro Irrigation Project to properly utilize the water resources without any wastage. Under the Drought Prone Are Programme, construction of 3540 watersheads was taken up in 11 districts. In Anantapur district where the drought conditions prevail in long spells of time, 772 watersheds are built to bring 3.31 lakhhs under cultivation.

IT and Technology

The new Industrial Promotion Policy, facilitating Foreign Direct Investments for setting up a number of major industries in the state. The Policy envisages several incentives to the industries. SemIndia Inc. and Government of Andhra Pradesh have signed MoU on February16, 2006 to promote $3 billion (Rs.13,500 crore) Fab City project in a 1200 acre land near Shamshabad for manufacturing Semiconductors/Microprocessor chips for computers, television sets, mobile phones and other digital devices, which is described as the single largest investment for decades to come, in hardware sector in the country. The Fab City is expected to provide employment to thousands of persons directly and also employment to thousands of persons directly and also indirectly. SemIndia Inc. plans to invest $1 billion in phase-I of the project within one year on the assembling and testing facility. The actual Fab facility for manufacture of wafers (chips or microporcessors) of different sizes will be completed in another 2 years after an additional investment of $2 billions. The state has already made large strides in software manufacturing by registering a 65% growth rate last year and in.

To promote Apprel Industry in the state the state government signed a MoU with Brandix Group of companies for setting up of an Apparel City in Visakhapatnam with a potential of 60,000 jobs over a period of 4 years. Similar Apparel Parks are proposed in Ranga Reddy, Chittor and in some other districts. A major Rs.6053 crore coastal districts infrastructure development scheme is posed to Ministry of shipping in Centre to take up under public-private partnership. The novel Project is expected to boost employment facilities in Vizianagaram, Srikakulam, Visakhapatnam and East Godavari Districts. The Project involves 10 new porst, improvement of minor ports, ship repairs facility, Promotion of coastal tourism and recreation facilities. Government is in the process of exploring the possibilities to set up industries using Bauxite reserves available in our state for creating employment opportunities to the youth, particularly among tribals. A Gems and Jewel Park is proposed by Gitanjali Group of Industries near International Airport which will provide employment to 50,000 persons over a period or 4 years. The government is keen to make use of natural gas available in Krishna-Godavari basin for the development of industry. A mega Jawahar Pharma City is coming up near Visakhapatnam involving estimated investment of Rs.182 crore in 2120 acres of are a will provide employment opportunities considerably. The latest issue of 'Garnier' magazine revealed that Andhra Pradesh is having the required potential and congenial atmosphere to achieve IT objectives of India by 2010. Sanctioning of sites for promoters for development of infrastructures for IT companies was effectively linked with generation of local employment potential, in the new IT policy. While in 2003-04 the increase in Software exports from the state is only 40%. The increase in IT exports went up by 64.5% worth Rs.8270 crore last year than that of the previous year. As many as 152 new Software Companies started production and the number of employees working in IT sector increased from 86,000 to 1,26,000. The state government is committed to using Information Technology for the benefit of all citizens especially those living in rural areas below poverty line. The launching of Rajiv Internet Village (Rajiv) programme during August 2004 is a step in this direction. This programmed envisages delivery of services to rural folk through a chain of 22,000 kiosks. With a view to capture 33 per cent of the national share in IT and Information Technology Enabled Services by 2009, the government has set up four 'Think Tank' for IT, Information Technology Enabled Services, Hardware and Animation. Based on the recommendations of these groups, a comprehensive and revised ICT Policy was brought out in January '05. this will accelerate the growth of Information Technology sector in the State with Tier-II cities like Visakhapatnam, Warangal Vijayawada and Tirupati emerging as key centers.

Industrial Programmes

The congress government had recognised the importance of large-scale industrialisation that can provide employment and higher incomes to the poor people. There it is committed to create a favourable investment climate for domestic and foreign investors in the state's industry and infrastructure. The government intended to give top priority to thrust sectors such as food and agro-industries, pharmaceuticals, biotechnology, tourism, technology and small-scale industries.

Industrial developmental strategy

To remove the existing barriers, create a free-investment climate and to make Andhra Pradesh a strong base for manufacturing sector several proactive measures are proposed by the government. These include infrastructure creation, investment subsidies, export promotion, attracting mega, and foreign direct investments, market access, towards better regulation, prevention of industrial sickness, exit policy, intellectual property rights etc.

Cluster development programme

Six industrial clusters were identified for development under "Industrial Infrastructure Up-gradation Scheme". Two clusters namely Pharma Cluster near Hyderabad and Auto Components Cluster in Vijayawada has already been approved by Government of India for assistance and they are in process of development. Four other clusters namely Marine food Processing Cluster in Bheemavaram, Power loom Cluster in Sircilla, Leather Cluster in Hyderabad and Precision Engineering Tools and Components in Ranga Reddy are under consideration by the Government of India. Apart from these, 14 more clusters are in the process of development under DCSSI assistance. Further, A mega Jawahar Pharma City is coming up near Visakhapatnam involving estimated investment of Rs.182 crore in 2120 acres which would provide employment opportunities considerably.

Sector specific economic zones

The authorised manufacturer of Adidas sports shoes, Apache Footwear, has signed a MoU to invest Rs 500 crore to set up a manufacturing facility in Nellore district of Andhra Pradesh. The unit is expected to employ 30,000 people over a period of four years. The state government has provided 314 acres of land to the company for the facility and production is expected to begin soon. This project will be developed as a sector specific special economic zone (SEZ) for footwear with all the necessary infrastructure facilities and the state government has extended all SEZ benefits to Apache. The company, in turn would provide housing facilities, super markets, a dispensary, schools, training institutes and transport to the nearby city for all the workers.

Hardware and nano parks

The government is inviting entrepreneurs to utilize the facilities that the state is offering to set up hardware manufacturing units. About 5000 acres were allotted at Samsabad for setting up hard ware park. The main objective of the park is to support the software operations in the country and attract MNC's and other IT giants to strengthen the country's status in the Information technology. Apart from the hardware park, another 3,000 acres near Shamshabad would be allotted for the proposed Nano Park. The state government has also decided to set up product-specific special economic zones in the hardware park for both hardware and software development operations.

Hyderabad has been selected as the location for India's first Fab City, a silicon chip manufacturing facility, being setup with an investment of $2billion by the AMD-SemIndia consortium. The proposed Fab-City with investment of about more than thousand crores, is expected to provide employment to thousands of people and shall facilitate billions of dollars of exports in next 10-years.

Bio-diesel project

World over research for alternative fuels is stepped up due to high prices, emission of green house gases and scarcity of the fossil fuels. Inorder to meet the fuel requirements, cost efficiency and lower the emission of gases, the Chief Minister, YS Rajasekhara Reddy had announced an ambitious project for taking up bio-diesel plantations of pongamia and jatropha over an extent of 51 lakh acres in the rain shadow areas in the next three years at an outlay of Rs.5000 crores. A state level Bio-Diesel Board has been constituted to oversee the implementation with the Chief Secretary as Chairman. It would be a tripartite activity involving the Government, the farmer and non governmental agencies with the AP Academy of Rural Development acting as nodal agency.

On the eve of world environment day, 2005, even a bio-diesel RTC bus was flagged off by Chief Minister Y.S. Rajashekhara Reddy.

Agro-industries

Andhra Pradesh holds the first rank in area and production of mango, oil palm, chillies and turmeric. It occupies second rank in citrus and coriander; third rank in cashew; fourth rank in flowers and fifth rank in grapes, banana, ginger and guava based on area and production. It holds second rank in livestock and meat production. Less than two per cent of meat is converted to processed product in spite of having second largest livestock of buffaloes and sheep in the country. Andhra Pradesh contributes about a third of country's egg and about one fifth of broiler meat production. But only few per cent of the total produce is processed. There is a large potential for production of a variety of processed products from the fruits and vegetables grown in the state. Therefore, a special package of incentives has been unveiled for the setting up of agri- processing industries.

Entertainment Industry

A new chapter, in the annals of the history of Telugu film industry, was opened by replacing the 20-year old 'slab system' for collection of entertainment tax from cinema halls in the limits of municipal corporations and special grade municipalities by rational collection of tax w.e.f April 3, 2005. The landmark decision would reduce the ticket rates by 30 per cent in higher classes thereby boosting the low budget cinemas.

Social Programs

As promised to the people earlier, Dr. Reddy kept his word to bring "Indiramma Rajyam" to the state, distributing 1.55 lakh acres of land to in a single day, 1.12 lakh landless poor, including S.Cs, S.Ts, B.Cs, the pattas of which were provided to the woman of beneficiary's family. On August 21st 2005,the Prime Minister Mr. Manmohan Singh launched the Second Phase of the Land distribution Programme, in which 1.68 lakh acres of land was distributed to about 1.06 lakh landless poor families. This mammoth programme is unique in the history of Andhra

Pradesh. In all,in two phases, more than three lakh acres have been distributed among the landless poor in the State.

Indira Prabha

To facilitate immediate and effective cultivation 3.23 lakhs of acres assigned to the poor, the State government has launched Indira Prabha scheme. The beneficiaries will get financial assistance from Indira Prabha to make their land cultivable.

Housing

Recognising the need to accelerate the tempo of the weaker sections housing programme, the government has embarked on a very ambitious plan to provide 40 lakh houses in 5 years as against the total of 49.64 lakh houses constructed since its inception under the programme, in a period of more than 2 decades. In all, 12,00,000 houses have already been completed since 2004. 1800000 houses are targeted during this financial year.

Indiramma

This scheme is intended to provide basic amenities to one-third of villages and one-third of wards in the urban areas. This scheme is implemented starting from 2006-07 for about 5 years. About 1.82 crores rural and 45 lakh urban population will be covered by 2009. Housing, drinking water supply, sanitation and drainage system, link roads, power connection to habitations and households, health services, AIDS awareness and prevention, nutrition and pre-primary education for children, pensions to old, widows and weavers and disabled are some of the areas the scheme would cover.

Rajiv Gruha Kalpana Padhakam

For low-income urban population, government has launched an innovative housing scheme, Rajiv Grihakalpa, with civil infrastructure and free land being provided by government. The government will provide Rs.30,000 towards the cost of land development charges. The beneficiaries should contribute 10 per cent of the remaining Rs.70,000. The rest of the amount would be arranged in the form of loans from banks.

Rajiv Yuvasakthi Padhakam

The Congress government launched a new scheme by name Rajiv Yuva Shakthi to provide wage employment and self employment to one lakh youth during 2004-05 with an outlay of Rs.321 crore. It also prepared an action plan for providing employment to 1.5 lakh youth with an outlay of Rs.624 crore during 2005-06.

Akshara Bharathi

As part of improving literacy levels in the State from the present 61.11 per cent, the Congress government launched another spell of *literacy programme 'Akshara Bharathi' in October, 2004.*

Bapuji Vignana Kendras

By converging the Open Schooling System, the network of libraries and Continuing Education Centres, government has started 246 Bapuji Vignana Kendras to facilitate the local people to obtain new information, new competencies and new skills.

JAWAHAR KNOWLEDGE CENTRES (JKC)

Jawahar Knowledge Centres (JKC) was set up in every district to impart industry grade (soft) skills to female engineering students to ensure their campus selection by the industry.

Indira Kranthi Padham

The activities of DWCRA and Velugu were integrated under a programme called Indira Kranti Padham. The basic objective of this integration is to implement various programmes for strengthening of self-help Groups with similar implementation strategy. The new scheme Indira Kranti Padham had been designed by clubbing Women Empowerment with Poverty Alleviation

Ambedkar Jeevana dhara

A new Scheme "AMBEDKAR JEEVAN DHARA" with an outlay of Rs.250 crore has been launched on Ambedkar's Birthday(Apr,14) to provide safe drinkig water to all Dalit habitations of even less than 500 population each.

Praja Patham

Praja Patham was launched on April 11, 2005 in order to ensure visits of all mandal level officers, along with concerned legisletor, to all panchayats and sort out problems in the areas of drinking water supply, housing & employment assurance etc.

INTEGRATED CHILD DEVELOPMENT SCHEME (ICDS)

In order to promote the concept of one girl child norm particularly in the rural areas (BPL families), the state government has decided to provide an insurance cover of Rs. 1 lakh to newborn baby girls. Families of below poverty line (BPL) having an annual income below Rs.25,000 are eligible for the scheme. The insurance amount will be paid to the girl when she attains the age of 20. The government will pay the premium to the Life Insurance Corporation of India.

Andhra Pradesh State Programme-wise Development
From May 2004 to May 2009

FIRST TIME IN THE WORLD

Item/Scheme	Achievement
Aarogyasri Insurance	Medical treatment costing Rs.2 lakh to seven and half crore including middle class people. 2 lakh surgeries as of now. A rare record in the world history. Treatment, Operations covering 942 diseases. March forward towards Total Health Andhra Pradesh.
104 Rural Mobile Health Units	Fixed Day Health Scheme through 104 mobile units to every village. 475 mobile health units availability to every village on a fixed day in a month. Free health checkups, free medicines for entire month, quality healthcare at the doorsteps of 4 crore rural people.

Pavala Vaddi	For the first time in the world, differential interest rates to women. Interest is 3% only. Applicable to farmers and weavers also.
Abhayahastham (IKP Life Insurance Scheme)	Monthly pension ranging from Rs.500 to Rs.2,200 to all women over 60 years of age. Life Insurance, Scholarships to their children. Only one rupee per day to be paid by the SHG members. Large scale benefit to One Crore 25 lakh women.
Projects	The life-line projects of Telangana region, "Pranahitha-Chevella" and "Devadula" are the world's second highest level water pumping Lift Irrigation Schemes.

FIRST TIME IN THE COUNTRY

Current charges, Taxes	Not single Paisa enhanced in current charges since the last five years. Oath taken in the Assembly, not to enhance for the next five years. No other tax was enhanced.
Additional power purhcases	Rs.6,500 crore expenditure during the past two and half years. The 40% growth in power demand is the indication of the tremendous progress made in Agriculture, Industry and Service sectors.
Rajiv Udyogasri. Jobs (Government and non-Government)	No Vacancy boards disappeared. Wanted Boards reappeared. 10 lakh jobs created in the past 5 years in Government and private sectors. Another 10 lakh jobs through Rajiv Udyogsri in the coming two years. 55,000 jobs in SEZs as of now. Ultimate aim is to create 25 lakh jobs. 11,000 vehicles utilised in one Jalayagnam programme alone. Direct and indirect jobs and employment to more than one lakh persons. 50,000 teachers as of now. 17,000 Police recruitment completed. Efforts are on for recruitment of 20,000 more police. 53,000 teachers recruitment would be completed in the coming 3 months. Training in Mason jobs to 38,000 unemployed as part of INDIRAMMA housing programme.

Jalayagnam (Irrigation)	Irrigated water provided to 19 lakh acres additionally as of now. 81 projects launched. 12 projects completed. Another 13 projects under completion. Remaining projects in fast progress by working day and night.
Free Power	Uninterrupted free power supply to 30 lakh pumpsets (families) since four and half years on record scale. 1500 crore units free power to Agriculture sector every year.
Agricultural Loans	Loans worth Rs.22,650 crore distributed in 2007-08. Rs.26,000 crore targeted for 2008-09. The interest rate is only 3%.
Farmers' loans waiver	Rs.11,100 crore loans waived to 64 lakh farmers, highest in the country. Rs.1,800 crore distributed by State Government @ Rs.5,000 as incentive to each of 36 lakh farmers who were not covered under loan waiver scheme announced by the Centre.
Land distribution	6.04 lakh acres distributed to poor... Rs.500 crore for land development. Six lakh acres Land ownership rights to Tribals.
Agricultural Labourers	All round benefit to more than one crore persons. Full stop to migrations. Daily wage enhanced from Rs.20 to Rs.82.3... Likely to be raised ro Rs.100. Top rank at national level in the implementation of National Rural Employment Guarantee Programme by using Social Audit, Smart Card and e-governance.
Pasu Kranthi	Purchase of 1,50,000 cattle at 3%interest and Rs.30,000 subsidy. White Revolution in villages.
Sheep Insurance	This scheme is being implemented in the State for the first time in the entire country.
Aarogyasri, 108 Ambulances	108 Ambulances are made available to all at all times. Ambulances were made to reach to any place in the State with in 18 minutes. Every day, 802 Ambulances with 6,000 emergency trips is a new record. Total Health safety to seven and half crore people through Aarogyasri.
104 Help Line	50,000 calls per day. Tele-medicine. Free Health information. Time to time counseling.

Houses	39 lakh houses were built since the past four and half years. 28 lakh houses under construction. Indiramma target is 80 lakh houses. With the construction of the remaining houses, Andhra Pradesh would emerge as the only State without huts in the coming two years. The housing budget rose 10 times from Rs.500 crore to Rs.5,000 crores since the last four years. Check to irregularities through 24 hour help line, quick response teams and social audit. House sites were distributed to more than 20 lakh poor.
Self Help Groups	More than One crore women Self Help Groups joined as of now.
Loans	Rs.16,535 crore since the past four and half years (By December 2008). This year target is Rs.11,000 crore. By March, 2009 the total loan distribution would be Rs.23,000 crore in five years period. The Government aims at making one crore women as lakhiers in the coming four years.
Micro loans-Total percentage in the country.	42 %. The lion's share out of the country's micro lonas is enjoyed by our State women only.
Cooking Gas	Ours is the only State that has bore the entire burden of Rs.50 on Gas enhanced by the Centre.
Ration Cards	An additional 50 lakh new white ration cards sanctioned as of now. Ration cards to all the eligible. White cards to around 2 crore families including the middle class.
Loan waiver	Rs.2,000 crore waived to beneficiaries who have taken loans through S.C., S.T., B.C., Minorities' Corporations.
Handloom Sector - Weavers	Rs.327 crore loans of handloom weavers waived. 3 lakh families benefited by loan waiver. Pensions to 1.5 lakh weavers. Budget rose to more than Rs.150 crore.

Andhra Pradesh State Programme-wise Development

From May 2004 to May 2009

Pensions	Since the last five years, new pensions to 55 lakh...By 1st of every month, 71 lakh pensions regularly @Rs.200 each.
Education	University in every district. 17 new Universities established apart from specialized Universities. Several new Universities like IIT, IIIT, BITS Pilani established.
Students Fee	For the first time in the country, 100% fee reimbursement to B.C., Minority, Poor among Upper castes (E.B.C) students including S.C. & S.Ts. Free Higher Education. Rs.2,500 crore allocation made towards fee reimbursement during 2009-10. 26 lakh students benefited as of now. 7 lakh EBC students would benefit additionally. With this Govt. will be bearing the burden of providing higher education to 85% of the students. (11 lakh B.Cs., 5 lakh S.Cs, 1.8 lakh S.Ts, 7.4 lakh minorities and 25,000 disabled...in total around 33 lakh students would benefit under the scheme.
Welfare Budget	In 2008-09, budget was allocated to welfare sector on a large scale at Rs,30,000 crore.
B.C.Budget	Rs.1,600 crore was allocated in 2008-09.
Minority Budget	Rs.200 crore allocated in 2008-09.
Mass Marriages	Mass marriages were conducted through T.T.D's Kalyanamasthu and to Minorities through Minority Department..
Development, Plan, Welfare sector, Capital Expenditures.	As per the latest R.B.I. Report, the State ranks 1st either in absolute terms or on percapita basis in development, plan, social, capital expenditures. Agriculture registered two digit growth rate in 2007-08 as no where else in the country.

FIRST TIME IN THE STATE

I.T. & I.T. Jobs.	New I.T. Policy formulated in 2005 for speedy progress and to reach top position in the country. Steps initiated for I.T. development in the cities like Visakhapatnam, Vijayawada, Tirupati, Warangal. 1,584 I.T. companies established as of now. 1.53 lakh jobs newly in I.T.sector. Rs.26,122 crore I.T.Exports in 2007-08
I.T.exports Percentage	Andhra Pradesh achieved 15% of the National exports. National growth rate is 32% and the State's growth rated recorded as 41%.
Industries	Fast industrialization in every district. Industrial development at cities like Visakhapatnam, Vijayawada, Tirupati and Warangal. According to R.B.I. report, our State ranked 2nd in the country in attracting investments in 2007-08.
Employment in Industries	Rs.16,700 crore investments from 2004 to 2008. 2.14 lakh jobs created. Some more industries being established and fast completing at a total investment of Rs.38,600 crore... aimed at creating 1.3 lakhs jobs.
Subsidy Rice	Rice made available to 2 crore families @Rs.2 per kilo only. Government is bearing more than Rs.3,000 crore towards Rice subsidy.
Essential Commodities	Rice, Red gram and palm oil monthly essential commodities being supplied at Rs.103 only.
Local Bodies Duties-Funds	Janma Bhoomi-Nodal Agency cancelled. Rs.6,110 crore spent in the last four years itself.
Production	Agricultural production with 199 lakh M.Ts is a major achievement. The State regained its lost glory as Annapoorna. Farmers are well off and brimming with confidence.
Minimum Support Price Percentage	Price rise and percentage in MSP in the last five years- Paddy-Rs.350 (64% raise), Cotton-Rs.1075 (56% raise), Jowar, Sajja, Maize Rs.355 (66% raise), Pulses Rs.1150 (84% raise), Ground Nut Rs.700 (50% raise) and Sunflower Rs.965 (77% raise).
Universities	Government took a policy decision to establish one University in each district. 18 new Universities established including Veterinary, Horticulture universities as of now.

Educational Institutions	New educational institutions like I.I.T, IIIT, BITS Pilani established. I.T.education being imparted in 1,000 schools and computers supplied to Madarsas.
Rural Education	World-class education being imparted in the Rajiv Gandhi Triple ITs to 6,000 rural students in I.T, Bio-technology, Nano-technology sectors. Free education to majority students. 11 Polytechnic colleges, 9 Junior Colleges, 31 Degree Colleges opened. As part of SUCCESS School education scheme, English Medium education with CBSE syllabus imparted besides computer training.
Jawahar Knowledge Centres	Training is being imparted to students of more than 1,000 vocational colleges as per the industrial needs, with the aim of creating employment to 5 lakh persons. Already training/placement provided to 60,000 students. Rural and backward class students are getting jobs employment in multi-national companies.
Community Colleges	Evening classes in Government Colleges/Universities...Diploma and Degree awards to working persons. Evening Polytechnic courses in the existing Engineering Colleges. Diploma seats in the State doubled. One I.T.I established in each of the constituency.
Education Budget	Rs.35,000 crore spent in the past five years.
Higher Education Budget	Rs.1,500 crore in 2008-09 and Rs.2,383 crore allocated for 2009-10.
Co-operative Sugar, Spinning Mills	5 closed Sugar Mills and 2 Cement plants were re-opened. The package of the State Government for merging BHPV in BHEL won accolades from employees and labour associations nation wide. Government jobs provided to 1,486 employees due to the closure of Allwyn based on their efficiency and utility. Pension facility to Allwyn employees on par with Government employees. Several Public Undertakings like APGENCO, RTC, Singareni company etc. are running in profit path with the support of the Government.

Rajiv Yuva Sakthi	80,000 youth trained in various sectors at a cost of Rs.21 crore. Rs.20 crore financial help extended to 4,540 weavers.
S.C.,S.T entrepreneurs	20% additional subsidy. Additional reimbursement at 0.25 paise on power unit. 25% additional reimbursement on Sales Tax. Separate Trust established through which the entrepreneurs would be provided guarantee.
Rains	For the first time in the history ...Full rains in five years. All dams full of water continuously for five years. Water flows to tanks what were not full in twenty five years and heavy flows to Singur project that has not witnessed full waters for eight years. Plenty of Agricultural production and hydroelectricity generation.

6

Tragic End

In the heart-rending tragedy of Yeduguri Sandinti Rajasekhara Reddy's death in a helicopter crash, Andhra Pradesh has lost its most charismatic leader and the Congress its most politically talented and resourceful Chief Minister. A medical graduate, YSR, as he was widely known, was inducted into politics by his father, Y.S. Raja Reddy, a shrewd politician of Pulivendula in Kadapa district who was murdered by rivals. YSR proved a quick study. He became an MLA at the age of 29, a Minister two years later, and never lost an Assembly or Lok Sabha election thereafter. A devout Christian, he made pilgrimages to Bethlehem and Tirumala with equal piety, showing his broadmindedness. The real surprise was his metamorphosis from a factional leader whose detractors dismissed him as a rebel without a cause into a party unifier. The game-changing event was his 1500-km padayatra in 2003, which brilliantly tapped into mass unrest over the agrarian crisis and catapulted him to the seat of power a year later. For five years and three months, YSR strode the State stage as the Strong Leader. There was no effective challenge from the Opposition or, for that matter, from within what used to be a notoriously faction-ridden State Congress. Such was his self-assurance that when he made it back to power with a wafer thin majority, he did not perceive any real threat to his pre-eminence. He had accomplished something extraordinary in post-1971 Congress affairs: emerged from the long shadow of the high command without raising doubts about his loyalty.

YSR was a strategic risk-taker who looked around eclectically for ideas that would be useful to him and initiated a plethora of welfare schemes to alleviate extreme economic distress among the rural and urban masses. His most impressive political achievements were the confidence and can-do spirit he injected into his camp and the political credibility he won for his schemes through incessant mass contact. His tenure, however, was marked by controversy, with a number of allegations of corruption and misuse of power levelled against him and his regime. He also showed signs of intolerance of criticism, which was revealed in his government's vendetta against the Eenadu group. YSR achieved the distinction of being the only Congress leader to serve a full five-year term as Chief Minister and was on course for a second full term. He tirelessly presented his mission as the transformation of agriculture and farmers' lives and the ending of agrarian distress. His 'Jalayagnam' drive to irrigate ten million acres of land by 2014, his Agriculture Technology Mission, his vigorous implementation and expansion of the National Rural Employment Guarantee Scheme, and his schemes to supply rice at Rs. 2 a kg to the poor and provide free power to farmers won him enormous credibility on the ground. His death at the age of 60 is the kind of loss the Congress will find extremely difficult to recover from.

Body Retrieved

A rescue helicopter retrieves one of the five bodies found on the hills of Nallamala forests near Kurnool in Andhra Pradesh on September 3. The bodies included that of Andhra Pradesh Chief Minister Rajasekhara Reddy. He was among the five persons killed when the State government's Bell-430 chopper crashed on September 2 in the morning.

Earlier, all hopes of Rajasekhara Reddy having miraculously escaped were snuffed out in less than two hours of the resumption of the search-and-rescue operations at daybreak. The operation involved a multi-disciplinary team of the Indian Air

Force, Greyhounds, the anti-naxalite force of Andhra Pradesh and others.

Based on aerial images, IAF choppers zeroed in on the crash site around 8 a.m. Evidence suggested that the Bell-430, laden with fuel for its long haul from Hyderabad to Chittoor, had crashed into a hillside between Atmakur and Rollapenta villages in Kurnool district and exploded.

As other choppers joined the operations, commandos slid down to the crash site. The wreckage was strewn over a wide area.

A 20-member team carrying stretchers, power saws and rope ladders reached the site and helped winch the bodies up the IAF helicopters hovering above. This brought to an end one of the largest land-and-air search operations launched in the country's history.

The mangled remains of Rajasekhara Reddy and the four others in the helicopter were flown to Kurnool, about 70 km away. Post-mortem was immediately conducted. Those who died along with Dr. Reddy were his Special Secretary P. Subramanyam, IAS; Chief Security Officer A.S.C. Wesley; and the pilots, Group Captain S.K. Bhatia and Captain M.S. Reddy. All the bodies were airlifted to Hyderabad.

Crash Site Shows Signs of Explosion

Death was possibly instantaneous for Y.S. Rajasekhara Reddy and four others, when their helicopter crashed into Pavurala Gutta, a steep hillock between Atmakur and Rollapenta villages of Kurnool district.

The chopper, which had veered 18 km off the set flight path possibly due to low visibility conditions, crashed into the hillock and burst into flames. "There was a black [burnt] patch spread over nearly 25 to 30 sq m, indicating that the chopper had exploded on impact," said an officer who monitored the search operations from here.

The helicopter was carrying enough fuel to fly for two more hours. When it took off from the Begumpet airport in normal weather conditions on Wednesday morning, the Bell-430 had fuel adequate for three hours of 'endurance'. The flight time to reach the destination, Anuppalle village in Chittoor district, was two hours and 20 minutes. It flew for nearly one hour.

The search operations resumed by Thursday morning. The IAF choppers pinpointed the 'latlong' coordinates of the crash site by about 8 a.m. The information was communicated to the base station set up in Kurnool, which in turn alerted the Greyhounds control centre here.

Within minutes another IAF chopper scrambled from Kurnool with Greyhounds commandos. By then the control here had alerted the commando units which were scouring the core area to reach the crash site.

There were nearly 20 units (each with 30 members) moving on either side of the Atmakur-Rollapenta road stretch at the northern tip of Kurnool district. Geographically, the borders of Prakasam district begin after Rollapenta on the southern side. Further north is Srisailam, which houses the holy Saivite temple. After this point starts Mahabubnagar district on the north. Down south, the Nandyal Reserve Forest area begins after about 6 km of plain terrain.

Informed sources said there were eight commando units on the northern side while eight were on the southern side of the Atmakur-Rollapenta road stretch. The other four units were at a distance of 7 km from the crash site. These four units were given the 'grid reference' and told to move to the site with the aid of GPS handheld devices. The terrain was extremely difficult, but identifying the target area was easier as IAF choppers were hovering over the crash site.

SMS Led Search Team to the Crash Site

A Short Messaging Service sent to one of the four mobile phones carried by the passengers of the helicopter that flew Andhra Pradesh Chief Minister Y.S. Rajasekhara Reddy led the search team to zero in on the area of the crash site.

"The SMS enabled those planning the search to zero in on the area to a four-km radius that finally resulted in the helicopters spotting the wreckage," official sources said here.

The SMS was received at 12. 06 p.m., nearly 90-odd minutes after the ATC lost contact with the helicopter flying the official team to Chittoor. This input, the sources said, meant the mobile phone was in an area where it could get some signal. And this helped in narrowing down the search area.

The mobile service provider furnished the details of the SMS received by one of the four mobiles to those coordinating the search.

The mobile which received the SMS presumably belongs to the security officer. Since the SMS was delivered through a tower, the coordinates were mapped on the basis of this input as well as data that the fighter aircraft and other IAF helicopters collected, the sources said.

The novel approach was adopted after the daylong search by IAF helicopters did not yield any result, forcing the IAF to deploy three Su-30 MKI aircraft, in two separate missions, to map the vast area.

The sources said the IAF headquarters received a request for help around 1.15 p.m. on September 2. Within 15-20 minutes, two Chetak helicopters from the helicopter training base at Hakimpet started conducting sorties.

Their effort was supplemented by another Mi-8 transport helicopter, which took off from Yelahanka, near Bangalore, to carry out a search based on the inputs given by the State government and the police.

At 4.30 p.m., the IAF launched a Dornier aircraft from Yelahanka, which flew to Kadapa, through Srisailam and Chittoor, before returning to the base.

Thirty minutes later, the IAF launched transport aircraft Avro from Hyderabad. The IAF opened an operation centre at Kurnool by 6.20 p.m., and by 6.45 p.m., it decided to press the fighter planes equipped with Synthetic Aperture Radar to map the area.

Two Su-30 MKI flew from Bareilly at 8.10 p.m. and returned to their base 10 minutes past midnight. The Il-78 transport refuel tanker was flown from Agra to back up the operation. At 2.15 a.m. on Thursday, the IAF launched its third Su-30 MKI, with another Il-78.

As the IAF did not have radar data, which it uses to locate wreckage of its planes, it decided to innovate. Based on the last contact the helicopter made with the ATC in Shamshabad and Chennai, it decided to search from the last point. The area was mapped, and the SMS helped in the process.

Two Chetak helicopters left for the area at 6.20 a.m. and at 8.28 a.m. spotted the wreckage. At 9.20 a.m., another Mi8 roped down two police commandos, and another three commandos slid down from an Advanced Light Helicopter. With the help of IAF personnel, the bodies were winched up to the helicopters.

Loved by Friends, Feared by Enemies

Late on Wednesday afternoon, a few hours after the chopper carrying Y S Rajasekhara Reddy went missing, intelligence officials had darkly indicated that the helicopter had gone down with an explosion. Around the same time, a senior police official from Kurnool district said, in an equally hush-hush manner, that the helicopter had landed in Veligonda region of Nallamala hills.

A day later, with news about YSR's death confirmed in the manner suggested by the intelligence officer and at the very same place revealed by the cop a day earlier, the big question is–was this a remarkable coincidence of two sharp speculations proving right or was there actual information that no one broke pending an official announcement?

Or perhaps the answer lies in the simple fact that YSR had emerged as such a colossus in the state, and so inspired awe and fear in equal measure, that nobody could muster courage to publicly articulate intelligent conjectures about his death. That this was the reason why misinformation was going back and forth on Wednesday about how Rajasekhara Reddy was found alive and taken to safety, only to be denied within minutes.

But it was not always like this. Although YSR was born rich he had no political legacy to fall back upon. He was a trained physician and practised for a while. More than that, he was a natural leader who came up in stages by the sheer dint of merit. He became an MLA in 1978 and a junior minister in 1980, but then was pushed into virtual oblivion for a long phase.

He became an MP and came close to Rajiv Gandhi, but before he could hold any important public office, Narasimha Rao was pushed to the PM's gaddi. The wily Rao recognized the potential of Reddy and decided to keep him down. The reputation of YSR's father Raja Reddy–a muscle man from Rayalaseema who had accumulated vast mining rights–had something to do with this attitude towards the son.

But YSR was himself not a muscle man. He was a strong man and had inherited streaks of his fathers flamboyant personality. That he came from the badlands of Rayalseema, where it rains very little and life is hard, toughened him as a young man. It nurtured in him a tremendous spirit of survival as well as inculcated intolerance towards forces hostile to him. For, YSR would destroy his enemies in a determined manner, bit by bit.

The goal mattered more than the means of decimating obstacles on his way, be it the Telangana movement or the Maoists.

If enemies feared him, friends absolutely loved him. For friends he was generous to a fault and would overlook their foibles-something like another successful politician, Chandrasekhar, who would never fight shy of owning up his friends even if they came in very dark shades of gray. In an illustrative example, some time ago when someone complained about the highandedness of his close friend, YSR is said to have remarked: ``He is my friend. When will he throw his weight around if not when I am the chief minister?"

Such support for his friends and his spontaneous show of affection bred strong loyalty for the man. His followers would rarely betray him, even if he fell on bad days. He was true to his friends and expected them to reciprocate. In that respect, YSR banded with his party men and lived by a code of basic honesty. Few questioned his integrity in human dealings and relationships.

This didn't necessarily extend to his material dealings, not at least in the eyes of his critics. For although he was re-elected on a development plank, and used public resources to shower largesse on electors, be it free power or free medical treatment, YSR displayed strong feudal tendencies.

Land was close to his heart and there were allegations that he had added to his estate in native Pulivendula by grabbing forest land. An unprecedented number of scams hit the state during his regime including the Volkswagen scandal in which the state government paid Rs 11.5 crore to the person masquerading as a representative of the German company.

Politically, YSR was astute. Having been in the bad books of Narasimha Rao, he realized that he had to be in the good books of 10, Janpath. And he could do this by proving useful to the high command. ``YSR realized that the Congress wanted seats in the

Lok Sabha and generous contributions to the party coffers. He worked hard for this and soon got in the good books of the powers that be," said a political analyst who knew the man from close.

If this was the way to the high command's confidence, it worked. Before his death, YSR had become so powerful that he was not a mere Congress CM. His stunning performance at the last Lok Sabha polls (no doubt with some generous help from Chiranjeevi), ensured two things–one, the Congress would be comfortable in Parliament and two, he could never be removed at will. In fact, it was said that if he were to be ever treated roughly or unjustly, he had the potential to break the state Congress and kick off an Andhra Congress.

In a state where N T Rama Rao came to power invoking insult to Telugu pride because Congress chief minister Anajaiah was berated by Rajiv Gandhi on the tarmac of the Begumpet airport this is the strong legacy that YSR leaves behind.

7

Condolences

Rajasekhara Reddy Was One of Our Most Charismatic Leaders: Sonia Gandhi

A visibly emotional Congress president Sonia Gandhi on led the Congress Party in mourning Andhra Pradesh Chief Minister Y.S. Rajasekhara Reddy, who played a key role in scripting the creation of the United Progressive Alliance in 2004 and its coming back to power this year.

Both Ms. Gandhi and Prime Minister Manmohan Singh acknowledged this in their brief remarks to the media after the Congress Working Committee (CWC) met in New Delhi. In its

Congress president Sonia Gandhi and Prime Minister Manmohan Singh come out after a Congress Working Committee meeting held in New Delhi on Thursday to condole the death of Andhra Chief Minister Y.S. Rajasekhara Reddy.

resolution, the CWC said Dr. Reddy's outstanding record of achievements as Chief Minister helped the Congress return to power in the State in May and "contributed to our remarkable victory in the Lok Sabha elections."

Referring to the recent Lok Sabha elections, Ms. Gandhi recalled how the Congress senior leadership was apprehensive of the party's prospects in Andhra Pradesh. "Every time, he kept telling us, 'Please trust me; I know the people of Andhra Pradesh, they will vote for us and we will surely come back'."

This confidence of Dr. Reddy has become part of Congress legend, as leaders privy to closed-door meetings remember him telling the high command that he would deliver 35 Lok Sabha seats to the party's kitty. He was not very off-target: the Congress won 33 seats, the highest the party bagged from any State.

Describing the Chief Minister as one of "our most charismatic leaders," she echoed the CWC resolution, stating his 'padyatra' ahead of the 2004 Assembly elections was instrumental in bringing the Congress back to power after a decade in the Opposition.

Reflecting the mood in the Congress since Wednesday when Dr. Reddy's helicopter went missing, Ms. Gandhi said: "We waited in hope day and night. We hoped he would be back on his feet alive. Sadly, we got this terrible news."

His Legacy Will Live On: Manmohan Singh

In a message to Vijayalaxmi Reddy, wife of Andhra Pradesh Chief Minister Y.S. Rajasekhara Reddy, Dr. Manmohan Singh said: "Rajasekharaji died as he lived–in the service of the people of Andhra Pradesh and the country.

In his untimely passing away, the state of Andhra Pradesh has lost an outstanding leader and the country has lost an ideal Chief Minister, who was a role model for other states."

On a personal note, Dr. Singh added, "I have lost a valued colleague, on whom I depended for support and ideas. Rajasekharaji's life was one of tireless commitment and service to the people, especially the poor and the underprivileged. His legacy will live on and will inspire many others in the time to come. "Your husband was a natural leader of men, who was loved equally by the public, his colleagues and the common man. The void his passing away has left behind will never be filled. My wife joins me in extending our heartfelt condolences to you and your family members. I pray to God to give you the strength and the fortitude to guide you in this hour of profound personal loss."

The Prime Minister said that under Dr. Reddy's stewardship, Andhra Pradesh became a role model for governance. A dynamic Chief Minister, he carried forward the idea, ideals and vision dear to the Congress.

Not Only AP but Entire Nation has Lost a Leader: President

President Pratibha Patil led the nation in mourning Andhra Pradesh Chief Minister Y.S. Rajasekhara Reddy, who died in a helicopter crash near Kurnool in Andhra Pradesh. In a message from Moscow, where the President was on a State visit, Ms. Patil described him as a dynamic Chief Minister, and said that in his death the people of not only Andhra Pradesh, but the entire nation, had lost a leader and that his loss would be deeply felt.

"I had the opportunity to interact with him on a number of occasions. During our interactions, his deep commitment to the development of Andhra Pradesh, its rural areas, and the weaker sections of society and empowerment of women was always evident."

The Country Lost a Towering Personality: Meira Kumar

Lok Sabha Speaker Meira Kumar expressed her deep shock and profound grief. "In Shri Reddy's passing away, the country lost a towering personality, who, till his last breath, struggled hard to safeguard the rights of the poor and the underprivileged and facilitated all-round development of the State of Andhra Pradesh."

She also condoled the deaths of Special Secretary P. Subramanyam, Chief Security Officer A.S.C. Wesley, and the two pilots, Group Captain S.K. Bhatia and Captain M.S. Reddy, who were with the Andhra Pradesh Chief Minister in the helicopter.

Reddy Will be Remembered for his Deep Empathy for the Poor: Hamid Ansari

Vice-President M. Hamid Ansari, said Dr. Reddy would be remembered for his personal qualities and modesty, his deep empathy for the poor and the downtrodden and for the rational changes he brought about in administrative matters in the State through an emphasis on the development of the rural economy alongside new and emerging technological sectors.

Son of the Soil: Rajnath Singh

Cutting across party lines, political parties and their leaders paid rich tributes to Dr. Reddy. Bharatiya Janata Party president Rajnath Singh called him "a son of the soil, who had a special concern for the welfare of the poor and other weaker sections of society."

AP Had Lost a Popular Leader: Advani

Leader of the Opposition in the Lok Sabha L.K. Advani said that in his death, the people of Andhra Pradesh and the country had lost a very able and popular leader of the masses. "His contribution to the development of Andhra Pradesh, particularly the deprived classes of society, is praiseworthy."

Nation had Lost an Illustrious Son: Gowda

Janata Dal (Secular) leader and former Prime Minister H.D. Deve Gowda said the nation had lost an illustrious son, an able administrator, a visionary, a statesman and a dynamic leader. "The fact that he lost his life, while on his way for a surprise check to a village, amply reflected his concern for the poor and the underprivileged."

Critical Loss to Farming World: Swaminathan

The untimely and tragic death of Dr. Y.S. Rajasekhara Reddy is a grievous loss to Indian agriculture at a time when the country needs most visionaries of his foresight and commitment to reverse the decline in farm productivity, profitability and sustainability. He was a true follower of the principle enunciated by Jawaharlal Nehru in 1947 that "everything else can wait but not agriculture." Soon after he became Chief Minister of Andhra Pradesh in 2004, he convened a meeting to formulate measures to end the then prevailing widespread agrarian distress. This led to a major thrust in irrigation under the Jalayagnam programme and the launching of an Agriculture Technology Mission.

Similarly, the first major step he took after his re-election as Chief Minister in June 2009 was to prepare a strategy to give the power and the economies of scale to farm families with small and marginal holdings through cooperative farming. He was unique among political leaders in the country in identifying the basic malady confronting agriculture, namely, inadequate attention to providing small and marginal farmers the best available technologies and services by mobilising the power of group cooperation through farmers' cooperatives, a management tool which led to the milk revolution in the country.

The fatal journey he undertook was also to ascertain whether all their entitlements reach the rural poor. The best tribute we can pay to his life and work is to carry forward his unfinished goals, the most important of them being the dawn of a life of hope and cheer among rural families, and ending agricultural decline and agrarian distress.

He Led from the Front: Governor

"Words fail me to give expression to my deep sorrow and anguish," A.P. Governor N.D. Tiwari said in his condolence message on the death of Chief Minister Y.S. Rajasekhara Reddy.

Mr. Tiwari described Dr. Reddy as a charismatic and dynamic leader who had endeared himself to the people with his deep commitment to their welfare and uplift. He led the State on the path of unprecedented growth and development. He always wanted the fruits of development to reach the common man. "The people of India will also remember him for his dedication to Gandhian ideals and values."

The Governor said: "Rajasekhara Reddy symbolised the aspirations of all the people of Andhra Pradesh and he stood resolutely for the development of its most backward regions. He led from the front and was an inspiring figure. It is most tragic that he had laid down his life while taking the administration to the doorsteps of the people."

Andhra's Lost a Good Leader, Me a Friend: Naidu

In Y.S. Rajasekhara Reddy's untimely death, Andhra Pradesh has lost a good leader. On a personal note, I've lost an old friend, said N. Chadrababu Naidu, the former Chief Minister of Andhra Pradesh.

Our careers moved parallel, the two of us becoming MLAs for the first time in 1978, serving as ministers in governments of T. Anjaiah, B. Venkataram Reddy and K. Vijaya Bhaskara Reddy.

Only that YSR became Chief Minister after me. He was first elected to the assembly as a candidate of the Congress faction led by Brahmananda Reddy after the Emergency. I won on the Indira Congress ticket. Later, he joined the parent party. Being from the same age group and the adjoining districts of Kadapa and Chittoor, we moved together. Till 1983 we were close friends and met almost daily. We visited Delhi together and often went to Tirupati for pilgrimages.

Thereafter, I joined the TDP when it was launched, laying the basis of our political battles. But we only fought on public and political issues. Between 1999-2004, he was the Leader of Opposition and I the CM.

In 2003, when Naxalites made an attempt on my life, he went on an impromptu dharna (sit-in protest) at Tirupati.

While the search operations were on, I was in constant touch with his son Jagan Mohan, State Finance Minister Rosaiah and Defence Minister Antony. I condoled with his wife and son after the news of his death.

A Progressive Leader: Vajpayee

Former prime minister and senior BJP leader Atal Bihari Vajpayee has condoled the death of Andhra Pradesh chief minister YS Rajashekhara Reddy, describing him as a progressive leader who was full of possibilities."The sad demise of Andhra Pradesh chief minister YSR Reddy has deeply shocked me. He was hard working, energetic, full of possibilities and a dedicated politician. In his death, Andhra Pradesh has lost a progressive leader," Vajpayee said in his condolence message.

Offering his condolences, Vajpayee said he prayed to God that Reddy's soul rest in peace and give his family the strength to bear the sorrow. Vajpayee also condoled the death of four others who were killed along with Reddy in the helicopter crash.

8

Important Speeches and Interviews

Speech At Thirteenth Finance Commission Meeting

Hon'ble Dr. Kelkar, Chairman, Dr. Indira Rajaraman, Prof. Atul Sarma and Dr. Sanjiv Misra, distinguished members and officials of the Thirteenth Finance Commission, my colleagues in the Council of Ministers and senior officers,

I deem it a privilege to extend you all a warm welcome, on behalf of the people of Andhra Pradesh. The spirit of co-operative federalism has been guiding the fiscal relations between the Centre and the States, despite differences in perceptions on a number of issues. Finance Commissions have played a major role in nurturing this spirit and in resolving contentious issues. Andhra Pradesh has always looked at the institution of the Finance Commission with great reverence and hope.

Many changes have taken place since the appointment of this Commission. The impact of the global meltdown, though not as severe as in most developed economies, has imposed an external constraint to the growth of our economy, which was well on its way to a higher growth trajectory. The enactment of fiscal responsibility legislations by the Centre and the States ushered in an era of rule based management of public finances. The considerable improvement in public finances in the last four to five years, facilitated by the higher growth of the economy, is now under threat. As part of the fiscal stimulus, there is a relaxation of FRBM targets. The State is already feeling the pressure on its finances, mainly on account of deceleration in the growth of its revenues and capital flows. The Thirteenth Finance Commission has a very difficult task on hand in taking forward the fiscal reforms further at this critical juncture. We are confident that under the able guidance of Dr. Kelker, the Commission would address the problems of States adequately.

To give you a brief background of the economic growth of our State since its formation on 1.11.1956, I would like to begin by quoting Sri B.P.R. Vittal, a Member of the 10th Finance Commission and a distinguished Civil Servant from our State. I quote

"The State was born with a congenital defect. It combined the less developed areas of the former States of Madras and Hyderabad. The princely State of Hyderabad itself has the lowest indices for human development in the South. In fact, A.P., at its formation was well behind the all India averages in respect of many parameters like per capita income, economic growth, human development, per capita power consumption, farm yields, literacy rates, population growth rates, per capita motor vehicles, number of villages electrified and life expectancy etc."

The successive Governments have, however, played a very significant role in building a modern, vibrant and dynamic economy for the State of Andhra Pradesh, ensuring growth with social justice in line with the broad economic policies pursued by the successive Governments at the Centre. During the first three decades, the Governments in the State have implemented many large and medium multi-purpose irrigation projects. Through a conscious effort, a very well diversified local technocrat entrepreneurial base was created. Many large industries were established both in the public and private sectors. We are leaders in sectors like Cement, Paper and bulk drugs, while having sizable presence in other sectors like fertilizers, steel, power equipment manufacturing, agro-processing, foundries and forging and the software.

Thanks to all the above initiatives, despite the initial handicaps and disadvantages, AP has caught up with other major states in terms of economic and social indicators and for the period 1981-91, AP's average annual economic growth rate at 6% was indeed higher than the national average. Agriculture grew at more than 4.5%. But, in post reforms period, more particularly during 1995-2004, the economic growth remained stagnant at 5.7%, lower than the national average for that period. The average annual growth rate in agriculture and allied activities fell substantially to 2.13%. There was unprecedented distress in agriculture and rural sector. For the first time, the State started witnessing suicides among farmers and other rural artisans. The fiscal position of the State too suffered heavily during this period. A State which had a cumulative Revenue Surplus of Rs.128 crores at the end of 38 years after its formation as on 31.3.1994, had suffered a cumulative revenue deficit of Rs.22,000 crores as on 31.3.2004, leading the State into what appeared to be an irretrievable debt trap, with the asset/liability ratio of the State declining to 63:100 from 101:100 as on 31.3.1994. The declining economic growth rate coupled with considerable fall in the real incomes of about 80% of State's population led to an unprecedented spurt in the extremist activities in the State.

When we took over the reigns of the State on 14th May, 2004, the immediate tasks before the Government were restoration of confidence among the farmers; restoration of confidence among the investors and lenders by reversing the trend of revenue deficits. The other major problem was about the extremist activities, which we believed could be eliminated only by increasing the economic growth rate.

The first thing that our Government did in 2004 was to implement a large number of programmes to immediately reach out to the farmers and other rural artisans who were in serious distress. These included waiver of the power dues of farmers, supply of seven hours free power to farmers, reschedulement of loans and interest, reduction in the rate of interest on crop loans, expanding the rural credit network etc.

The top priority, however, was to step up the economic growth in the State, as we firmly believe that faster economic growth is the only remedy for faster reduction of poverty. As higher economic growth is directly proportional to the level of investments, particularly the public investment, we have straight away taken many initiatives for stepping up the public investment on irrigation, weaker section housing and other infrastructure projects like sea ports, airports, power generation, SEZs and development of coastal corridor. The Plan Expenditure of the State went up from Rs.11,794 crores in 2003-04 to Rs.41,539 crores in 2008-09 recording a compounded annual growth rate of 28.63% which is perhaps the highest growth rate for any State in the country. In absolute terms our Plan Expenditure in each of the last four years has been the highest for any State in the country. Similarly, the Capital Expenditure went up from Rs.4,250 crores in 2003-04 to Rs.13,697 crores in 2008-09, registering an annual growth rate of 26.37%. The capital expenditure as percentage of fiscal deficit for the period 2004-08 increased to 150% as against 45% during the period 1994-2004.

Again, as in the case of Plan Expenditure, AP's Capital Expenditure in absolute terms is the highest for any State in the country. As private investments always grow in proportion to the public investments, there was an overall spurt in the investments in the State in an unprecedented manner, leading to the highest ever economic growth rate of 9.1% for the five years period 2004-09, higher than the national growth rate of 8.5% for the same period. Higher economic growth and higher economic buoyancy in the State have lead to a phenomenal increase in the revenues of the State, which grew during 2004-09 at 18.2% per annum as against 13.51% recorded for the period 1999-2004. The revenues to GSDP ratio for the year 2007-08 have gone upto 16.48% in the year 2003-04.

With the revenues of the State registering a healthy growth, the Government implemented a large number of welfare schemes to benefit the poorest of the poor like never before not only in our State but in any other parts of the country. We have provided good and health security to about 80% of the State's population. Our women SHG program is one of the best in the world. 50% of the Country's Bank lending in this sector is in AP. This has helped substantially in unleashing their potential and their growth as leaders. This is one of the biggest State supported programs. Again for the first time, recognizing that education is a powerful tool for social empowerment, the State has implemented a scheme for complete reimbursement of tuition fess in an unprecedented manner to benefit more than 20 lakh post metric students belonging to BC, SC,ST and Minority communities in the State. The weaker section housing programme and the pension scheme to the old aged, disabled, widows etc., are by far the largest social security measures ever taken by any State in the country. As per the latest report of RBI on State finances for the year 2008-09, AP stood first in the country in respect of its allocation on Plan expenditure, development expenditure, social sector expenditure and capital expenditure.

Our greatest performance was, however, in agriculture, although for the last five years, we have done a commendable job even in industries sector by achieving an annual growth rate of 10%, as against Country's growth rate of 8.8%. In agriculture and allied activities, as against the national target of 4% annual growth rate, our State achieved a very high growth rate of 6.4% for the period 2004-09, up from 3% growth rate for the preceding five years period. In quantitative terms, AP's food grains production recorded an average annual growth rate of 8.98% for the period 2004-09, as against the nation's 1.9%. We have contributed 84 lakh tones of rice to the national pool in the last year and this is approximately 60% of our rice production. This became possible because of our investments in irrigation and free power policy for farmers. Our Jalayagnam programme covering about 81 irrigation projects with a capital outlay of Rs.1.76 lakh crores to provide assured irrigation to about 100 lakh acres besides providing stabilization to 21 lakh acres is the biggest initiative in the country in the post independence era. We have been supplying more than 1500 crore units of free power annually catering to about 60 lakh acres. We firmly believe that as long as the subsidies go towards enhancement of production and increases in the rural incomes, they cannot be considered populist.

The biggest challenge our Country is facing today is the low growth rate in agriculture and stagnated productivity levels, contributing to perpetuation of low levels of incomes for about 60% of our population. Unless we do something very substantial for improving farmers' incomes, in the long run, we cannot achieve sustainable growth, let alone inclusive growth. Besides, with our population growing more than 2 crores per annum and the global tradable surplus in foodgrains coming down because of developing countries converting their lands to bio-fuel crops, augmenting additional domestic foodgrains production becomes the top priority. In recognition of this alarming position, the Government of India launched the National Food Security mission in 2007, although belated. As there has been no major technological breakthrough in agriculture in the last two decades, the only way we can increase the productivity and consequently the farmers' incomes is by making more water available to farmers. This is precisely what we are doing. I can assure you that this initiative will go a long way in meeting our country's food security on the one hand and improvement of incomes of 60% of our population, which is of paramount importance to all of us.

I strongly urge that the Finance Commission should give a very high weightage in devolution of central taxes to the states implementing irrigation projects and augmenting additional goodgrains production. You may also kindly consider a special grant for Irrigation projects in our State, as they contribute more towards the National Food Security than of our State. I request you to also consider coming up with a mechanism of sharing a part of our expenditure on free power for agriculture as that too is going towards contributing to national food security. We cannot simply afford to go back to PL 480 days. As we have seen, from our own experience, the capital investments on Irrigation Projects will have an all-round beneficial impact on the economy. Because we are implementing a large number of irrigation projects and weaker section housing programme, the cement and steel industries in our State have doubled their capacities. With the result, the construction, transport and mining sectors have experienced high growth rates of over 15% per annum in real terms in the last five years. The virtuous cycle of economic growth was fully operational in our State.

Nevertheless, we are no exception to the ongoing global economic slowdown. As per the recently revised CSO data, our State, which registered an annual GSDP growth rate of 10.08% in constant terms for the four years period 2004-08, as against national growth rate of 8.92%, has to content with just 5.6% growth rate for the year 2008-09, because of global economic slow down. Consequently, the financial resources too fell sharply. Although our final accounts for the year 2008-09 are not yet ready, as per the latest estimates, revenue receipts are likely to fall short by Rs.8,000 crores from the budgeted estimates, while there will be a short fall of Rs.10,000 crores on account of capital receipts. This is quite a big resource gap. The enhancement of fiscal deficit eligibility to 4% is a small concession. The need of the hour is to raise resources and spend it on capital asset creation (infrastructure), even if it means a little rise in inflation figures in the short run. We cannot afford to allow our economy to get into a morass. The 13th Finance Commission should give a serious thought on how to make more resources available to States like ours which are already in the mid-way in the implementation of a large number of Infrastructure projects. Keeping them on hold for whatever reason is not in the National interest, as after all, the GDP of the country is the sum total of the GDP of all States.

Another important submission is with regard to the fiscal deficit. The 12th Finance Commission in its wisdom has fixed the limit of 3% of GSDP for fiscal deficit, which broadly means the net borrowings of the States for the year. The borrowing limits should have a bearing and proportionality to the repayment capacity, which is more a function of revenue receipts. As revenue receipts to GSDP vary from State to State, allowing all States to borrow at 3% of their GSDP is perhaps not correct. For instance, both Andhra Pradesh and West Bengal have the same population and same GSDP of Rs.3.50 lakh crores. But our revenues are Rs.62,000 crores as against their revenues of Rs.35,000 crores. As per the present policy, both AP and West Bengal can raise the same level of loans, although AP has better repayment capacity and should naturally have higher borrowing limit. I request to look into this anomaly and come up with a more rational basis for fixing the borrowing limits.

There are varying estimates about the gas availability in the KG basin. The RIL has already started commercialization of gas from their D6 block. The first land fall point for the gas in KG basin is East Godavari District of Andhra Pradesh. It is unfortunate that our State does not get any share in the royalty or in the profit share. We do not enjoy any priority in allocation nor in pricing. This is completely unjust. The extreme interpretation of the Constitutional provisions about the offshore resources should not be invoked to deny the people of our State their due share. The 13th Finance Commission is requested to address this important issue.

Coming to the subject of Central devolutions, I have a few submissions to make. There has been an increasing trend towards centralization as seen from the reduction in the share of State Plan outlays, increasing number of Centrally Sponsored Schemes, cesses and levy of surcharges. I request that the declining trend of Finance Commission transfers be arrested. The vertical distribution of resources has to be based on responsibilities. I request you to consider compensating States in case of delays in the fixation of royalties on major minerals. I also request for realignment of resources in favour of States accomplishing the objective of inclusive growth. Further, I request that the States' share of Central Taxes be raised to 50% from the present 30.5%. Finally, I request you to kindly provide incentives for better performance and investments in infrastructure.

I request that the following weights may be assigned in the distribution formula:

1. Population 30 per cent.
2. Area 15 per cent.
3. Per capita income distance 20 per cent.
4. Tax effort 10 per cent.
5. Infrastructure and social sector expenditure 25 per cent.

I am aware that Dr. Kelkar has actively championed the introduction of the GST, based on the concept of Grand Bargain. GST is soon going to become a reality. I request you to ensure that the Finance Commission will provide a fool-proof mechanism for compensating states for the possible loss of revenues in the first few years after migration to the new system. We firmly believe that tax devolutions should be the main channel, while grants have to become residual. Needless to say, the grants should focus more on improving the quality of expenditure, filling the gaps in basic and specific needs of States. I request you to consider State specific grants for our flagship programmes like Aarogyasri, Jalayagnam, Rural Water Supply and others as detailed in the Memorandum.

The presentation to follow will no doubt highlight a large number of issues and this will be followed by discussions. One final word, please help progressive States like ours with more funds; we will give back several times more to the Country, as we have demonstrated during the last five years. I am grateful to you for your time.

Jai Hind

(Chief Minister Dr. Y.S. Rajasekhara Reddy's Speech at Thirteenth Finance Commission meeting on 20.7.2009.)

My Government Committed To Economic Reforms: YSR Reddy

You are a frequent visitor to Delhi nowadays, isn't it?

Not very frequent. But at least once a month.

But that's sometimes a problem with the Congress chief ministers?

Well, Delhi is the national headquarters. Government of India is put up here. So, coming once a month I don't think is out of turn.

But, it's often said for Congress CMs that they have to keep coming to Delhi for everything, even transfers, postings.

No, absolutely not. But, we are a national party, we are not a regional party and anything important, we keep Delhi apprised of. If we have to take their permission, we do take. We know how to work in a national party.

But, you are one of the particularly fortunate CMs for two reasons. One, you lead one of the very few governments which are entirely dependent on Congress' own MLAs. They don't have any coalition partners to worry about and second, you ran this campaign and won and you built it over many years.

No, the first part is right. We have 190 MLAs. We don't need to depend on anyone else. Out of 294, if we have got 191 MLAs, more than two-thirds MLAs we have. But the other part, running the campaign and all that, yes I did my best but it was the Congress party's campaign and all of us in the state and, of course, our leader Sonia Gandhi.

So, you can't take the credit yourself. Although I'm sure many of your colleagues will give it to you.

No, that's not right. No one in the Congress party can say that it is all because of me. Congress party's approach is different, the party's culture is different, the heritage is different. We believe in working together, taking the credit or even the discredit together.

A very different thing about you and your political career is that in a party which is sometimes run by very senior people, you became a party president at a very young age of 32.

When I was 33. It was because of Rajiv Gandhi. Rajiv's eyes fell upon me, he recognised me.

And how did that happen? Do you remember?

In one or two interactions with him, he thought that I'll be a proper person at that time to head the state congress party because I was quite young, he was impressed with my age, with the way I put things.

And your medical degree, I suppose.

My educational background. Somehow, Rajiv got impressed with me. I would not say all credit to my side, but he got impressed and he made me the state president. And since then, I never looked back.

And this in a state which had so many 'senior' leaders. In fact on a Walk The Talk with Sonia Gandhi, I had mentioned that sometimes her front row in Parliament looks like the ICU without the tubes. So, did you feel a generation gap?

That way, Congress party is definitely better than BJP or Communists. Well, national parties do have this problem. We can't ignore the experienced people, the elderly. But at the same time, we don't shy away from bringing in new blood into the system.

But, did you feel a generation gap in the state? Because all your leaders were in the 70s.

Yes, I did. Generation gap was there. There was a little resentment in the beginning. People thought how can a PCC president be only 33 years old. But, Rajiv was a totally different kind of a person. He did encourage the youth and because of that a new generation came into the party.

Yes, in fact people like Chidambaram, Kamal Nath, Gehlot, Digvijay. These are all people who came in around that time and have now become leaders. Do you remember any incidents of this resentment? From Narasimha Rao to Venkataswamy to Chenna Reddy, you had stalwarts of the Congress party.

I had some problem with Chenna Reddy.

Do you remember something that he said someday to you, "You young fellow, stay in your limits"?

Not exactly that way. He walked out of the Congress party and when the press asked me about his going out of the party, I a little inadvertently said, it was good riddance.

Those are things you don't say in the Congress party and then what happened?

Then the party high command said that inspite of him going out like that, you are not supposed to talk like that.

But the interesting thing is that your rival in the state is also your age, Chandrababu Naidu.

Yes, we are the same age. In fact we were together in Youth Congress, right from 1975 till '83. Until 1983 when

Chandrababu's father-in-law became CM and left the party to join his father-in-law.

And do you think until then he believed in Congress values?

In fact from '78 to '82, we were MLAs. Especially between '80, '81 and '82, we were also ministers in Congress party. We contested the '83 elections as Congress nominees. I won and he lost. And in that election, Telugu Desam won the state. His father-in-law, NT Rama Rao, became the CM and three days after that he told that there was pressure from home front and he wanted to change the party. I was really taken aback when he said that. What is this, Babu, till three days back, you were a minister in Congress party. The power is lost, fine but it doesn't mean that you go along with the power.

So, was it a pressure of power or pressure of the family?

I don't know. He said that there was pressure from the party. I advised him against leaving the party but on the third day he left the party.

But, he said something very interesting lately. He's now explaining his own loss of power to you. He is saying that the alliance with the BJP cost them a great deal. Do you sympathise with him, agree with him?

Maybe, he's now thinking that the BJP is not that important for him. But in the last elections, in 1999, when he won, BJP won that election. There was a pro-Vajpayee wave in the country. And he did win because of the BJP at that time.

But the last one he lost because of the BJP, you are saying?

I don't think so.

Then, why is he saying this now? Does he want to distance himself from the BJP? Because we already have the Left reaction. Jyoti Basu has already said that he's going away from the BJP and that the Left should welcome him.

If you ask me about Chandrababu Naidu's nature, I think he's an absolute opportunist.

I think it is inevitable that you will roll-back, when will you roll back free power to farmers? Deshmukh did that after you and he's rolled back in Maharashtra.

Unfortunately, Maharashtra doesn't have a system like ours in the power sector. In spite of the free power, Andhra Pradesh Electrical Utilities have got the best of Crisil ratings.

Crisil is the rating agency?

Yes, Crisil is the rating agency. In fact between last year and this year, our transmission and distribution losses have come down another two per cent. Earlier, it was 23 per cent, now it is 21 per cent.

Some of it might be because of the reforms that Babu talked about?

Fine, reforms are good if they can do things like bringing down transmission and distribution losses. We are not against reforms. We never said that we are against reforms.

But this was a good thing he did?

Bringing in reforms in the power sector was a good thing he did. And we are following it up in a more dynamic way.

So, how much free power are you giving and to how many people? Is it really benefitting people or is it just a slogan?

It absolutely benefits. In fact, last one full year, we gave free power to all the 23 lakh farmers and there was demand for more connections, so we thought we'll target out of these 23 lakh people. Whosoever are paying income tax, whosoever are big farmers, about five per cent of these people need not get free power. So, this year we are continuing to give free power to 95 per cent of the farmers.

You must be the only chief minister who says he can afford to give free power?

We are able to give. Absolutely no problem. And it is really helping the farmers.

And Maharashtra is no lesson to you?

Maharashtra has got its own problems and we have got our own problems and our own strengths. So, ultimately what we have to see is that if a farmer needs free power at a particular time, we have to help him.

So, you see it as a temporary measure?

At least for these five years, since we took the people's mandate on this.

It's like NTR's Rs 2/kg rice.

No, it's not that way. If by next polls, the conditions of the farmers are a lot more improved and at that time we feel that we can charge the farmers, we will tell the people that this is what we will do in the next term if when we get re-elected.

But still you don't see it as a permanent thing, subsidising agriculture through free power. It is unsustainable?

Basically, as and when it is necessary, it has to be subsidised.

So, you will keep reviewing it?

Yes, we will keep on reviewing it.

But in my books it is like Rs 2/kg rice.

The basic difference is that that's an unproductive sop. This is a productive sop.

How much extortion is now going on in your countryside by Naxalites?

A rough estimate made by the department was, in the first five or six months we gave them an opportunity to talk and police action was suspended, a rough estimate is that about Rs 50-60 crore has been collected by them and they did produce good weapons, they did plant landmines in a number of places. Well, it's part of life and you get used to it.

But are you feeling let down that they misused your ceasefire?

To some extent, yes.

Was it a betrayal?

You can call it that if you want but originally when the talks started, we did say that the issue of arms has to be discussed. It was included as item number 5 in the agenda. But they did discuss about other aspects but when it came to arms they said that we'll come and discuss it the second time. But in the meantime, they tried to arm themselves. Okay, that's what they thought. They wanted to use this opportunity to strengthen themselves.But in a democracy, for a strong government like ours, it's not difficult. We'll be able to maintain the law and order situation.

So, what's the solution now? Will you go after them or will you maintain a status quo?

Well, it's not a matter of going after them. It's a question of trying to win them over, win their cadres and ultimately if some kind of a situation can be managed where they will not have a breeding ground.

Why did you let go of their leadership when the police had them surrounded? It is a mysterious incident. You had them in a jungle, you had them surrounded and you let them go. It gave the impression that your government was in league with them and there was some kind of a secret understanding.

It was not a question of letting them go. But the situation was such that if we would have gone ahead, the senior Naxalite leader, maybe he would have got killed. But when the process of dialogue was still not discontinued, we thought let's give them a chance.

But it did demoralise the police because they thought that once we had them in our bag and the politicians let them go.

Nothing like that. In a democracy, we have to find ways and means of how we can get the best of the situation.

But did you take that decision?

In fact it was not mine. The Home Minister was contacted. At that time, I was in China.

You were not contactable then?

I was not contactable then. But the government, by and large, stands by whatever the government did.

But law and order being a state subject, in a crucial situation like this, how could the decision be left to the Centre? If you were a non-Congress CM, you would never have allowed this.

I'm talking about my home minister not the Central government.

The impression here was that the decision was taken at the highest level in Delhi.

No, no. In fact the people in Delhi were not contacted.

Our impression was that the PM's office was contacted. It was decided politically that it would be very uncomfortable if the entire top Naxalite leadership got wiped out in one operation.

It was not that way. Centre had nothing to do with that.

I hope they believe you. But how have they paid that gratitude back? I believe, they are killing a lot of people, including those they suspected of having informed the police of their whereabouts that day.

Looks like their attitudes don't change so easily. They are coming together with the Maoists. Their attitudes are more different. As long as they were separate entities, their attitudes were different.

And describe that change that you saw.

They did one absolutely cold-blooded killing in a village called Vempetta. The villagers were called to the forests, on the assumption that some kind of mediation is going to take place between two warring groups in the village and these people were taken one after another and killed in cold blood. This sort of thing had never happened in Andhra in the history of the extremists.

There was an article by K Bala Gopala alleging that you gave your blessings to many killings and violence and your father himself was a victim of political violence. He died because of that.

That article is a completely concocted article. I don't want to comment anything on that. My father getting killed in a faction violence is totally different. Two years earlier to that, some Telugu Desam people were attacked by some Congress people in a neighbouring village and the Telugu Desam people wanted to take revenge on the Congress leadership.

So, that's how you say your father got victimised?

That was as simple as that.

But there is a lot of political violence in Andhra, between Congress workers, TDP workers.

Unfortunately in the area called Rayalaseema, factional violence has been there for the past 80-90 years.

Are you trying to control that now?

Yes. Totally in control now.

Are you telling the TDP also to bury the hatchet and stop the violence now?

In fact, in the recent Penukonda by-election, it was a feud between two families, one belonging to Congress and one belonging to TDP. Till now, one Congress sitting MLA and three Congress ex-MLAs got killed in that place. One Telugu Desam sitting MLA got killed recently. In fact, I made an offer to Chandrababu Naidu that let's get out of this situation completely. Let's not give tickets to either of the families. Chandrababu didn't come around. But we stuck to our guns and decided that we won't give the ticket to this warring family, we gave the seat to a reconstruction man.

But you believe that this hatchet has to be buried now. This blood-feud can't go on now.

Should be happily buried and we are doing our best to make it happen.

Is that what you see as a priority now? To take away this shadow of violence–Naxalite or this factional violence.

I'll definitely try and do my best in this regard.

(Interview with YSR by Shekhar Gupta, Editor-in-Chief of The Indian Express)

Reforms Can't Be A Dogma

Congress workers from every section of society throng the Andhra Pradesh Secretariat eager to meet Chief Minister Y.S. Rajasekhara Reddy, popularly known as YSR. Having led the party from the front, he is clearly the hero of the Congress' spectacular electoral triumph. His master stroke was the 1,500 km-long padayatra that he undertook across Andhra Pradesh in May 2003, well before elections were announced. The medical doctor-turned-politician who hails from the Rayalaseema region was instrumental in focussing attention on the plight of farmers in the State. It is widely believed that the Congress campaign succeeded because it struck a chord with the mass of peasantry, which still remains mired in an unprecedented crisis, exemplified by the spate of suicides by farmers in the State.

Soon after assuming office, Rajasekhara Reddy got on with the task of implementing the electoral promises made by the Congress. His first act, soon after taking oath, was to waive the electricity dues of farmers and to provide free power to farmers in the State. Although he believes that his predecessor,

N. Chandrababu Naidu, has ruined State finances, he said that his first priority is to provide support to farmers in distress. In an interview he listed the government's priorities, problems and tasks. Excerpts:

During your campaign you highlighted the extreme distress of large sections of the people. How do the issues, particularly those related to the agrarian crisis, fit into your priorities now?

Our priorities will be the following: Agriculture, rural development, irrigation, industry, power and employment. We are not against industry. Nor are we against IT [information technology] or biotechnology. Basically, it is a matter of fact that in 1993-94 agriculture contributed 26 per cent of the State's gross domestic product (GDP). And, 67 per cent of the people in the State depended on this sector for their livelihood. In 2003-04, agriculture contributed only 13 per cent of the State's GDP. This is the reason behind so many farmers' suicides in the State.

It appears that the government has to provide immediate relief to farmers. But long-term measures may also be needed to tackle the problem. What steps are you planning to prevent suicide by farmers?

On every front we are doing everything that is possible. Immediately after coming to power we kept our promise of providing free power to farmers. We also kept our promise to waive almost Rs.1,200 crores dues from farmers for power. We are planning some strong proactive measures. Most of the suicides are because of failed irrigation systems, mainly because of the non-completion of projects. In the next five years, we plan to spend Rs.36,000 crores on such projects. These will extend irrigation to 65 lakh acres. These measures will also stabilise another 20 lakh acres which are already under irrigation.

How do you plan to mobilise the funds for these projects, the power subsidies and other measures?

We will need about Rs.46,000 crores for these measures. We will definitely be able to mobilise the funds. We are already in the process of doing this. Last year, the State government spent just Rs.900 crores on major irrigation works. The average annual expenditure on the measures I mentioned works out to about Rs.9,200 crores over the next five years. Where is Rs.900 crores and where is Rs.9,200 crores? We have already started making efforts to mobilise these funds. I am sure we will be able to provide at least Rs.6,000 crores to Rs.7,000 crores this year for these measures.

We have almost finalised a loan of Rs.2,000 crores from the Life Insurance Corporation of India (LIC). Despite the serious debt burden, Andhra Pradesh has never failed in its (repayment) commitments. And, we are clear that all the money we borrow will only go to finance projects, mostly irrigation-related. This means that the impact will only be on the fiscal deficit, not the revenue deficit. We will try and correct the revenue deficit. The State has a revenue deficit of almost Rs.3,000 crores. Our objective is to substantially reduce this.

At least seven to eight districts are in the rain shadow area. These constitute almost 30 per cent of the State's area. We are planning to create extensive bio-diesel plants in these areas. This will change the ecology of the area. We are also planning extensive micro-irrigation (drip irrigation) systems in these areas. For all these we need money. We intend to make sure that every paisa that we borrow goes into activities that promote development. We intend to involve oil companies such as Indian Oil Corporation and Reliance Petroleum in these projects. We plan to bring about 40 to 50 lakh acres under such plants in the next three to four years.

In the run-up to the elections you promised to review several projects, particularly the power-related ones. How far will you go on this issue? The issue is significant because it has a bearing on how much the government will be able to save so that it can cover the deficit on account of providing free power to farmers...

Oh! Yes we will review these projects. In the next three to four weeks you will see the results.

How many power purchase agreements (PPAs) are under review?

Three PPAs are being reviewed. A review of these three will enable us to cut costs substantially. The Comptroller and Auditor-General (CAG) of India pointed out that the costs were too high. The CAG said that two PPAs signed by the government with Spectrum Power and the GVK Group were costlier by at least Rs.200 crores when compared to other power generation projects. Since I assumed office, some of these managements are ready to scale down fixed costs of the power plants, which will result in lower tariffs.

Since last May, when you went on a padayatra, and particularly during your election campaign in association with the Left, the World Bank's conditionalities figured prominently...

The Left's ideology is slightly different from ours. We are not against reforms. We are also not against the World Bank. But they have some conditionalities which are not pro-poor. Sometimes they work against farmers. We know that the agricultural sector gets attention from the government even in the U.S., Japan and Europe. But when we give some free power to farmers, there is a hue and cry. We have to tell the bank that this is not correct, that so many farmers are committing suicide. Is it not a fact that something has gone terribly wrong? We have to tell the Bank that such things have to be reviewed. Reforms cannot be a dogma.

What about industrial activity? So many units have closed down in Andhra Pradesh...

That will be a major thrust area. We will make every effort to revive small industrial units. Capital worth thousands of crores is lying idle. Industrial units in the State are not able to compete because of two major factors. One, the cost of power is too high here. Secondly, the cost of finance is high. We want to subsidise the interest cost of small units. We have promised interest rates of 3 to 5 per cent to small units. This interest rate will be related to prompt repayment by borrowers. The government will bear the burden arising out of the subsidy that it will offer these units.

In order to do many of the things that you have promised the electorate, you will need the support of the Centre.

The Centre is an immense help to us. Our leaders in Delhi regard Andhra [Pradesh] as a special case. They have said that the Andhra Pradesh farmer should be given free power.

There has been a spate of suicides by farmers in the State in recent weeks. How are you tackling the issue?

The farmer is not a beggar. But if he is in a bad shape, is it not the duty of the government to help him? Some of the deaths in recent days are not really suicides, but natural deaths. We have started helplines for farmers. In the past six years, Andhra Pradesh accounted for three out of four farmer suicides in the country. Chandrababu Naidu did not address the reasons for the distress.

Is there not an immediate need to intervene to prevent suicides by farmers? Will the government declare a moratorium on debt repayment by farmers?

In the past two weeks we have been monitoring this on an everyday basis. We have had half a dozen meetings on this subject. No, we have not decided to declare a moratorium on repayments.

We Are The Champions

Chief Minister Rajashekar Reddy illustrates how Hyderabad is becoming a leader of IT and ITES in India. An enviable 64.5 per cent growth rate in software exports, it is a way ahead of the national average of 35 per cent during 2004-05. I would start by accepting the fact that our achievements so far, in the IT sector is just the beginning. The inroads made by Andhra Pradesh in the IT sector are spectacular with the global giants making a beeline for its capital Hyderabad. Not only Hyderabad, the wave is spreading to the hinterlands as well.

Companies like Satyam, Wipro, ilabs , Kenexa and Visual Soft are vying for space in Vishakhapatnam even as we keep a keen eye on other areas such as Vijaywada, Warangal and Tirupati in a focussed way. The industry-friendly atmosphere of the state is coming handy for huge investments in IT sector and there is no doubt that Hyderabad has emerged as a final point for the IT evolution. The state government with its pro-active efforts has shown its will to transform the state into a prime investment destination and the fastest growing economy in the country.

With the growth of 51 per cent during 2005-06 in software exports it is clear that Information Technology could retain its top position for the state for the second year in the row. In terms of absolute figures in IT exports, the state continued to be in the fourth position in the country, next only to Karnataka (Rs.37,500 cr), Maharashtra (Rs.15,500 cr) and Tamil Nadu (Rs.13,960 cr).

One more illustration to our significant growth is an enviable 64.5 per cent growth rate in software exports, which we are glad to announce that it is a way ahead of the national average of 35 per cent during 2004-05. It would be worthwhile to recall that the average growth rate of all IT & IT-enabled services companies in the country during the year was only 36 per cent.

With several top IT giants like Microsoft, TCS, UBS, Connexant, Cognizant, Amazon, Patni, Qualcom, Sonata, Wipro, Infosys and Honeywell to name a few expanding their network in Hyderabad a real boom in IT sector is all set to take place. If you take a look at the recent report on IT exports it shows that Andhra Pradesh could keep the pace of progress in the sector with a high rank by maintaining the standards both in terms of quality and quantity.

Global companies around the world have been lured to invest in Hyderabad by the timely and pro-active steps initiated by the efforts of the state government. It should be mentioned that the steps taken by the state government in promoting software industry through its innovative IT policy has starting bearing rich fruits and the rich dividends reaped by it only reinforce our commitment to do more for this sector.

Our vision has it that with our relentless efforts we soon will overtake Bangalore to become number one IT hub of the country. With several top IT giants like Microsoft, TCS, UBS, Connexant, Cognizant, Amazon, Patni, Qualcom, Sonata, Wipro, Infosys and Honeywell to name a few expanding their network in Hyderabad and Visakhapatnam, a real boom in IT sector is all set to take place which will place Andhra Pradesh heads and shoulders above anyone else in making it the real IT haunt.

Facts speak for themselves as our state stands among the top 10 industrialized states in the country with an investment of Rs.75,391 cr after Maharashtra (Rs.1,02,432 cr) and Gujarat(Rs. 78,696 cr) as per the recent analysis of Centre for Monitoring Indian Economy (CMIE) as on January 2006. It could now be said with propriety that Hyderabad has the potential to become a global outsourcing centre with a sustained growth in all sectors and services with regard to the huge available potential in the form of human resources.

If we look at the following records about IT exports one learns that overall exports from India during 2005-06 were to the tune of Rs 1,00,809 crore. However in terms of growth rate of exports, we feel enthusiastic to state that Andhra Pradesh was far ahead of others. For example while Karnataka and Maharashtra registered a growth rate of only 34 per cent, Tamil Nadu recorded only 29 per cent, as against 51 per cent growth rate achieved by Andhra Pradesh. Let us talk of investments made in the state. If the previous government could attract only Rs. 3,533 cr during its seven-year rule, I am pleased to state that the present government has attracted Rs 4,341 crore in the first year and Rs. 7,363 crore in its second year.

Not only that, look at our feat at the employment front. At present, about 1,60,000 IT professionals are employed in 1,382 companies in the state. We are not sitting still on our achievements attained so far, as the government has set the target of Rs 69,000 crore for IT exports and employment for more than

3.5 lakh IT professionals by 2009, particularly the rural youth. I am very confident while stating that in the coming years Andhra Pradesh would not only show impressive growth rate in IT exports, both in terms of percentage and absolute figures but will also retain its top position.

(Interview with Financial Express)

The Farmer Is My Lord

Dr Y.S. Rajasekhar Reddy has given interviews to many newspapers and T.V. Channels on the occasion of completing two years at the helm of affairs. "The welfare of the farmer is my aim. Every morning my first phone call will be to enquire on the farmer's problems. I discuss the ways and means of improving the farmer's life with the Minister, officials and many others as well. They are always in my thoughts'–these were his words. "The main reason for the desire for a Separate Telengana State has been the total neglect of them during the TDP regime. Those people started the separate state slogan only because there was neglect in the areas of industry and irrigation. But, they can now clearly see the development since we came to power. We will develop Telangana in such a way that they will believe such a development cannot be possible even in a separate state". He said he succeeded in making his own mark in the administration in the past two years. He said there was all-round development in the State. He mentioned that he had great respect for the Party High Command as well as the people. He was confident that they would be victorious in the Panchayats on par with the municipal elections. Here are some excerpts from the interviews:

Q: You are accused of giving importance only to irrigation projects and not other areas. What do you say?

A. It is true that we are giving importance to irrigation. Similarly, we are also giving importance to welfare measures.

Under Indiramma Project, we are building 18 lakhs houses in just one year. We are building latrines for the poor. We are giving old are pensions and widow pensions on a large scale. We are also offering loans to women organizations for a meager interest of 25 paisa.

Q: Though agriculture has definitely improved in the past two years, the allegation is that only the middlemen have benefited from it.

A: The farmers have actually got remunerative rates. Especially last year we saw that corn had a fantastic rate. We bought them through the Dwakra groups. Dwakra women have gained much experience in the sale of corn. We saw to it that middle men did not enter into this transaction. But with the entry of free trade, it is inevitable that middle men enter into it. Still, the government would directly enter the market to protect the farmer and see to it that he gets remunerative rates.

Q: Though the crop was good, the prices of pulses have gone sky high. What action is the government taking in this regard?

A: The rates of essential commodities are increasing. But the government has already bought certain commodities like tamarind and red gram and stored them. At the time of increase in prices, we will distribute them through public distribution system at reasonable rates. We are also trying to bring down the price of chilies. As you know, the government has a double duty to provide remunerative rates to the farmer as well as see that the consumer is not burdened.

Q: There is a rumor that the World Bank is insisting on withdrawing the Free power to farmers?

A: We are sincerely implementing the free power scheme for the welfare of the farmers. There is no question of bowing down to anyone in this regard.

Q: There is also a criticism that you are insisting on attaching capacitors for agriculture motors?

A: Capacitors are meant for the benefit of the farmers. Once you have capacitors, low voltage would not create problems. There will not be power breakdowns. Government is giving loans to buy capacitors through co-operative banks. Since we are explaining the benefits of capacitors, the farmers themselves are coming forward to acquire them.

Q: What action are you taking for the development of Information Technology in the State?

A: My government is taking special interest for the development of Information Technology areas. Because of our attempts, we are able to get crores of rupees in capital. Especially, many software companies are establishing their offices here. And this will provide lakhs of people with job opportunities.

Q: How is it possible to have smooth administration when so often there are misunderstandings and fights between Ministers-burocrats and senior officers-department heads?

A: It is quite natural for ministers and officials to be at loggerheads. But these are not serious. They are not affecting the administration. As for dissension between senior officials... well, that is also not new. It's been happening since ages. Still, we are making changes and modifications whenever necessary.

Q: Recently Parliament member Lagadapati Rajagopal, M.L.As P. Janardhan Reddy and Marri Sasidhar Reddy have been blatantly and openly opposing government policies? What do you say to this?

A: You very well know that our party is highly democratic. Everyone knows that these things are common in the congress party. No need to take them seriously.

Q: What do you think the outcome of the Panchayat elections would be?

A: Just like in the Municipal elections, here too, I am confident, we will be successful.

Q: Are you planning for seats adjustment with your allies?

A: At the Centre, Left Parties and TRS have supported the Congress on the basis of secularism. Since there has been no change in that stance, our party will have seats adjustment with Left and TRS in local elections.

Q: Narendra is saying even YSR cannot stop separate Telengana?

A: I am not bothered with the comments of the Telangana Rashtra Samiti leaders. They have their own way of thinking. I never said I would stop Telangana, nor did I say I would bring Telangana. The main reason for this demand has been the neglect of Telangana during the nine year TDP rule. The desire for a separate state grew because of the neglect of irrigation and industry. Now you can see for yourself the growth since we came to power. We will develop it to such an extent that people will believe even a separate State would not be able to accomplish.

Q: What does the refusal of Rajya Sabha seat to KVP Ramachandra Rao signify? Is it not a warning to you?

A: The High Command decided that his services are more essential at Hyderabad than at Delhi. We always respect the advice of the high command. Even if the High command does not send warnings, we do accept their warnings. We are very much aware of our limitations. We don't think that the Chief Minister is someone like the Nizam of Hyderabad. We have utmost respect for the High Command..., same with the people. We have the same respect for the media.